SELECTED POEMS

Andrew Young
Selected Poems

Edited by Edward Lowbury and Alison Young

CARCANET

This edition first published in 1998 by
Carcanet Press Limited
4th Floor, Conavon Court
12-16 Blackfriars Street
Manchester M3 5BQ

A CIP catalogue record for this book
is available from the British Library
ISBN 1 85754 392 0

The publisher acknowledges financial assistance
from the Arts Council of England

Set in 10pt Garamond Simoncini by Bryan Williamson, Frome
Printed and bound by Antony Rowe Ltd, Eastbourne

Acknowledgements

We are grateful to Brian North Lee for permission to reproduce Joan
Hassall's wood engravings, and to the Hunterian Art Gallery, University of
Glasgow, for permission to use *Ben More, Mull, from Iona*, by S.J. Peploe.

Contents

8

Foreword

The poetry of Andrew Young has been out of print for some years. Following the recent publication of a critical biography of the poet an increased demand for his work is to be expected, a demand in particular for a new edition containing his most famous poems. This new selection starts with an almost complete reprinting of the five books of what he called his 'canon' of short poems, illustrated by the fine wood engravings which Joan Hassall made for his *Collected Poems* of 1950. These are the poems of which C.S. Lewis said, 'there has been nothing so choice, so delicate and so controlled in this century'. Young had, in his maturity, discarded the romantic, discursive and convivial attitudes of his earlier poems, which did not suit him well, and developed a terse, wittily paradoxical and descriptively evocative style, a landscape with virtually no people in it, which was truer to his nature. The effect has more in common with the Metaphysical poetry of Herbert and Vaughan than with that of the Georgians. The 'canon' of short poems is followed by *Into Hades*, which shows that this master of the miniature could focus a similar imagination and wit to create a visionary and powerful long poem. After *Into Hades* we have placed a few of the best poems from Young's early books which were not 'quarried' (his term) for later use, and which show his emerging personal idiom. One poem from his first collection (1910) shows that in spite of the prevailing influence of Swinburne Young had a very unSwinburnian talent for concise description. There follow a few poems which appeared in his prose books and in letters. The volume ends with four prose poems from *The New Poly-Olbion* which show how Young identified extreme conciseness as a hallmark of what he looked for in a poem and hoped to achieve in his own poetry.

from

Winter Harvest
(1933)

The Flood

The winter flood is out, dully glazing the weald,
The Adur, a drowned river, lies in its bed concealed;
Fishes flowing through fences explore paddock and field.

Bushes, waist-deep in water, stand sprinkled here and there;
A solitary gate, as though hung in mid-air,
Waits idly open, leading from nowhere to nowhere.

These bushes at nightfall will have strange fish for guests,
That wagtail, tit and warbler darkened with their nests;
Where flood strays now, light-headed lapwings lifted crests.

But soon comes spring again; the hazel-boughs will angle
With bait of yellow catkins that in the loose winds dangle
And starry scarlet blossoms their blind buds bespangle;

Dog's-mercury from the earth unfold seed-clasping fists
And green-leaved honeysuckle roll in tumbling twists
And dreams of spring shake all the seeds that sleep in cists.

O blue-eyed one, too well I know you will not awake,
Who waked or lay awake so often for my sake,
Nor would I ask our last leavetaking to retake.

If lesser love of flower or bird waken my song,
It is that greater love, too full to flow along,
Falls like that Adur back, flood-like, silent and strong.

An Old Road

None ever walks this road
That used to lie open and broad
And ran along the oakshaw edge;
The road itself is now become the hedge.

Whatever brambles say
I often try to force a way,
Wading in withered leaves that spread
Over dead lovers' tracks a sighing bed.

Is it the thought of one
That I must meet when most alone
That makes me probe a place like this,
Where gossamer now gives the only kiss?

I shall see no one there
Though I had eyes to see the air,
But at the waving of a bough
Shall think I see the way she went but now.

The Last Leaf

I saw how rows of white raindrops
    From bare boughs shone,
And how the storm had stript the leaves
    Forgetting none
Save one left high on a top twig
    Swinging alone;
Then that too bursting into song
    Fled and was gone.

Killed by a Hawk

I stir them with my stick,
   These trembling feathers left behind
To show a hawk was sick,
   No more to fly except on the loose wind.

How beautiful they are
   Scattered by death yet speaking of
Quick flight and precious care
   Of those great gems, the nest-eggs, warm with love.

Feathers without a bird!
   As though the bird had flown away
From its own feathers, fired
   By strange desire for some immortal spray.

Winter Morning

All is so still;
The hill a picture of a hill
With silver kine that glimmer
Now whiter and now dimmer
Through the fog's monochrome,
Painted by Cotman or Old Crome.

Pale in the sky
The winter sun shows a round eye,
That darkens and still brightens;
And all the landscape lightens
Till on the melting meadows
The trees are seen with hard white shadows.

Though in the balk
Ice doubles every lump of chalk
And the frost creeps across
The matted leaves in silver moss,
Here where the grass is dank
The sun weeps on this brightening bank.

The Old Tree

The wood shakes in the breeze
   Lifting its antlered heads;
Green leaf nor brown one sees
   But the rain's glassy beads.

One tree-trunk in the wood
   No tangled head uprears,
A stump of soft touchwood
   Dead to all hopes and fears.

Even the round-faced owl
   That shakes out his long hooting
With the moon cheek-a-jowl
   Could claw there no safe footing.

Riddled by worms' small shot,
   Empty of all desire,
It smoulders in its rot,
   A pillar of damp fire.

The Green Woodpecker

Whether that popinjay
   Screamed now at me or at his mate
I could not rightly say,
   Not knowing was it love or was it hate.

I hoped it was not love
   But hate that roused that gaudy bird;
For earth I love enough
   To crave of her at least an angry word.

The Beech

Strength leaves the hand I lay on this beech-bole
  So great-girthed, old and high;
Its sprawling arms like iron serpents roll
  Between me and the sky.

One elbow on the sloping earth it leans,
  That steeply falls beneath,
As though resting a century it means
  To take a moment's breath.

Its long thin buds in glistering varnish dipt
  Are swinging up and down,
While one young beech that winter left unstript
  Still wears its withered crown.

At least gust of the wind the great tree heaves
  From heavy twigs to groin;
The wind sighs as it rakes among dead leaves
  For some lost key or coin.

And my blood shivers as away it sweeps
  Rustling the leaves that cling
Too late to that young withered beech that keeps
  Its autumn in the spring.

Loch Luichart

Slioch and Sgurr Mor
Hang in the air in a white chastity
Of cloud and February snow
That less to earth they seem to owe
Than to the pale blue cloud-drift or
The deep blue sky.

Though high and far they stand,
Their shadows over leagues of forest come,
Here, to a purer beauty thinned
In this true mirror, now the wind,
That held it with a shaking hand,
Droops still and dumb.

As I push from the shore
And drift (beneath that buzzard) I climb now
These silver hills for miles and miles,
Breaking hard rock to gentle smiles
With the slow motion of my prow
And dripping oar.

The Shadow

Dark ghost
That from tree-trunk to tree-trunk tost,
Flows with me still,
When on the shoulder of the hill
The late sunrise
Tangles its rainbows on my eyes –

Although
Each time I wave to you below
I see you stand
And wave back with a distant hand,
I ask, Can you be mine,
O shade gigantic and divine?

The Forest of Dean

'Now here you could not lose your way,
Although you lost it', seemed to say
Each path that ran to left or right
Through narrowing distance out of sight.

'Not here, not here', whistled a thrush
And 'Never, never', sighed a thorn-bush;
Primroses looked me in the face
With, 'O too lovely is this place'.

A larch-bough waved a loose green beard
And 'Never, never', still I heard;
'Wayfarer, seek no more your track,
It lies each side and front and back'.

In December

I watch the dung-cart stumble by
   Leading the harvest to the fields,
That from cow-byre and stall and sty
   The farmstead in the winter yields.

Like shocks in a reaped field of rye
    The small black heaps of lively dung
Sprinkled in the grass-meadow lie
    Licking the air with smoky tongue.

This is Earth's food that man piles up
    And with his fork will thrust on her,
And Earth will lie and slowly sup
    With her moist mouth through half the year.

March Hares

I made myself as a tree,
No withered leaf twirling on me;
No, not a bird that stirred my boughs,
As looking out from wizard brows
I watched those lithe and lovely forms
That raised the leaves in storms.

I watched them leap and run,
Their bodies hollowed in the sun
To thin transparency,
That I could clearly see
The shallow colour of their blood
Joyous in love's full flood.

I was content enough,
Watching that serious game of love,
That happy hunting in the wood
Where the pursuer was the more pursued,
To stand in breathless hush
With no more life myself than tree or bush.

The Stars

The stars rushed forth tonight
Fast on the faltering light;
So thick those stars did lie
No room was left for sky;
And to my upturned stare
A snow-storm filled the air.

Stars lay like yellow pollen
That from a flower has fallen;
And single stars I saw
Crossing themselves in awe;
Some stars in sudden fear
Fell like a falling tear.

What is the eye of man,
This little star that can
See all those stars at once,
Multitudinous suns,
Making of them a wind
That blows across the mind?

If eye can nothing see
But what is part of me,
I ask and ask again
With a persuasive pain,
What thing, O God, am I,
This mote and mystery?

A Man with a Horse

I wondered at the mighty horse
   So meekly since the day began
Toiling to make himself a corse,
   And then I wondered at the man.

The Spider

A single white dewdrop
That hung free on the air sang, Stop!
From twig to twig a speckled spider,
Legged like a hermit-crab, had tied her
Invisible web with WELCOME
For sign, and HOME SWEET HOME.

That spider would not stir,
Villain of her Greek theatre,
Till as I heedlessly brushed past her
She fled fast from her web's disaster
And from a twig-fork watched it swing,
Wind tangling string with string.

Now she weaves in the dark
With no light lent by a star's spark
From busy belly more than head
Geometric pattern of thin thread,
A web for wingy midge and fly,
With deadly symmetry.

The Round Barrow

A lark as small as a flint arrow
Rises and falls over this ancient barrow
And seems to mock with its light tones
The silent man of bones;

Some prince that earth drew back again
From his long strife with wind and mist and rain,
Baring for him this broad round breast
In token of her rest.

But as I think how Death sat once
And with sly fingers picked those princely bones,
I feel my bones are verily
The stark and final I.

I climbed the hill housed in warm flesh,
But now as one escaped from its false mesh
Through the wan mist I journey on,
A clanking skeleton.

Late Autumn

The boy called to his team
    And with blue-glancing share
Turned up the rape and turnip
    With yellow charlock to spare.

The long lean thistles stood
    Like beggars ragged and blind,
Half their white silken locks
    Blown away on the wind.

But I thought not once of winter
    Or summer that was past
Till I saw that slant-legged robin
    With autumn on his chest.

The Rat

Strange that you let me come so near
    And send no questing senses out
From eye's dull jelly, shell-pink ear,
    Fierce-whiskered snout.

But clay has hardened in these claws
    And gypsy-like I read too late
In lines scored on your naked paws
    A starry fate.

Even that snake, your tail, hangs dead,
    And as I leave you stiff and still
A death-like quietness has spread
    Across the hill.

The Star

A white mist swathed the valley;
    Each huge uncertain tree
Came looming through the darkness
    An island in a sea;
But when I climbed to Hawkley
    The stars held all the night,
Spangles and glittering ouches
    And clouds of hollow light.

I thought they were blest spirits
        Borne upward on a wind
And the white mist the cerements
        That they had left behind;
And you, your body sleeping,
        In their bright numbers moved
And with raised face I questioned,
        Which is my well-beloved?

The Men

I sat to listen to each sound
Of leaf on twig or ground
And finch that cracked a seed
Torn from a limp and tarnished weed
And rapid flirt of wings
As bluetits flew and used as swings
The bines of old man's beard,
When suddenly I heard
Those men come crashing through the wood
And voices as they stood,
And dog that yelped and whined
At each shrill scent his nose could find;
And knowing that it meant small good
To some of us who owned that wood,
Badger, stoat, rabbit, rook and jay
And smoky dove that clattered away,
Although no ill to me at least,
I too crept off like any stealthy beast.

After the Funeral

Standing beneath the jewelled trees
That waved with slow mournful unease;
I lifted up my eyes to them –
The stars caught in the trees' dark stratagem.

But when I asked which is the wonder,
All stars above the earth and under
And in the vast hollow of space
Or the stern look on that defeated face;

I said, 'Not even the Milky Way
Shines like the golden streak of clay –
All, all of her that I could save –
My foot has gathered from her open grave'.

The Burnt Leaves

They have been burning leaves,
Dead leaves the little shrew upheaves
Poking in winter for his trifling food,
And large black pools lie in the wood
As though the sky had rained down ink;
It all means nothing as I think
That more and more are left behind
To rise and rustle in the wind,
That paws them as a cat plays with a mouse,
And June will bring green leafy boughs;
Yet often as I watched them run
I thought of you, O blue-eyed one,
Or thought about my thoughts of you,
Fitful and feeble too:
For as these ran a little way and stopped
When the wind rose and dropped,
So I would think of you a little, yet
So soon forget.

In Moonlight

We sat where boughs waved on the ground
But made no sound;
'They cannot shake me off,'
Shrieked the black dwarf,
Impudent elf,
That was the shadow of myself.

I said to him, 'We must go now';
But from his bough
He laughed, securely perched,
'Then you rise first';
It seemed to me
He spoke in wicked courtesy.

We rose and 'Take my hand,' he whined,
Though like the wind
Each waving bough he leapt;
And as we stept
Down the steep track
He seemed to grow more hunched and black.

Loch Brandy

All day I heard the water talk
From dripping rock to rock
And water in bright snowflakes scatter
On boulders of the black Whitewater;
But louder now than these
The silent scream of the loose tumbling screes.

Grey wave on grey stone hits
And grey moth flits
Moth after moth, but oh,
What floats into that silver glow,
What golden moth
That rises with a strange majestic sloth?

O heart, why tremble with desire
As on the water shakes that bridge of fire?
The gold moth floats away, too soon
To narrow to a hard white moon
That scarce will light the path
Stumbling to where the cold mist wreathes the strath.

A Barrow on the Quantocks

Each night I pass the dead man's mound
I keep on turning round;
I almost stumble on the track
With looking back.

Although that mound of ling and stones
May hide his brittle bones,
I do not think that there he sleeps
Or wakes and peeps.

He is too intimately near
To see or touch or hear;
I only feel my blood is crossed
By his chill ghost.

It may be that all things are made
Of substance and of shade
And such a hill as I walk here
He walks elsewhere.

I know not which the substance is,
This hill of mine or his,
Nor which of us is the true ghost
In shadows lost.

The Roman Wall

Though moss and lichen crawl
    These square-set stones still keep their serried ranks
Guarding the ancient wall,
    That whitlow-grass with lively silver pranks.

Time they could not keep back
    More than the wind that from the snow-streaked north
Taking the air for track
    Flows lightly over to the south shires forth.

Each stone might be a cist
    Where memory sleeps in dust and nothing tells
More than the silent mist
    That smokes along the heather-blackened fells.

Twitching its ears as pink
    As blushing scallops loved by Romans once
A lamb leaps to its drink
    And, as the quavering cry breaks on the stones,

Time like a leaf down-drops
    And pacing by the stars and thorn-trees' sough
A Roman sentry stops
    And hears the water lapping on Crag Lough.

On White Down

In a high wood,
Wind chilling my premonitory blood,
I play at death
Closing my eyes and holding back my breath.

Ah glad surprise
To wake from death, and breathe, and open eyes
To see again
This mist-capped hill that is so bright with rain.

But from a bough
A blackbird mocks, 'Blind eyes are not enough;
You act the ghost
With sight and breathing that you never lost.'

O bird, be still;
When I would walk on an immortal hill
You drag me back
As though I had not left this dim hill-track.

The Farmer's Gun

The wood is full of rooks
That by their faded looks
No more on thievery will thrive,
As when they were alive,
Nor fill the air with the hoarse noise
That most of all is England's pleasant voice.

How ugly is this work of man,
Seen in the bald brain-pan,
Voracious bill,
Torn wing, uprooted quill
And host of tiny glistening flies
That lend false lustre to these empty eyes.

More delicate is nature's way
Whereby all creatures know their day,
And hearing Death call 'Come,
Here is a bone or crumb',
Bury themselves before they die
And leave no trace of foul mortality.

The Yellow-Hammers

All up the grassy many-tracked sheep-walk,
   Low sun on my right hand, hedge on my left
   Blotted by a late leaf, else leaf-bereft,
I drove my golden flock.

Yellow-hammers, gold-headed, russet-backed,
   They fled in jerky flight before my feet,
   Or pecked in the green ranks of winter-wheat,
While I my footsteps slacked.

Myself, the road, the hedge, these flying things,
   Who led, who followed as we climbed the hill?
   Loud as their repeated trembling trill-trill
Was the swift flirt of wings.

So tame I would have touched them with my hand,
   But they were gone, darting with rise and fall;
   I followed, till at the hedge-end they all
Dispersed over the land.

There, where the hillside scattered the sheep-walk,
    Deserted by the birds I stood to muse
    How I but now had served so sweet a use,
Driving my golden flock.

The Evening Star

I saw a star shine in bare trees
That stood in their dark effigies;
With voice so clear and close it sang
That like a bird it seemed to hang
Rising and falling with the wind,
Twigs on its rosy breast outlined.

An obvious moon high on the night
And haloed by a rainbow light
Sounded as loud as silver bell
And trees in flight before it fell,
Their shadows straggling on the road
Where glacier of soft moonlight flowed.

But moon nor star-untidy sky
Could catch my eye as that star's eye;
For still I looked on that same star,
That fitful, fiery Lucifer,
Watching with mind as quiet as moss
Its light nailed to a burning cross.

The Pines

The eye might fancy that those pines,
With snow-struck stems in pallid lines,
Were lit by the sunlight at noon,
Or shadow-broken gleam of the moon;
But snowflakes rustle down the air,
Circling and rising here and there
As though uncertain where to fall,
Filling the wood with a deep pall,
The wood that hastens darkness to hide all.

The hurricane of snow last night
Felled one; its roots, surprised by light,
Clutch at the air in wild embrace;
Peace like an echo fills the place
Save for the quiet labour of snow,
That falling flake on flake below
The torn limbs and the red wounds stanches,
And with a sheet the dead trunk blanches,
And lays white delicate wreaths among the branches.

Illic Jacet

This was his little house;
   Its moth-bright eye
Looks through the orchard-boughs
   At the starry sky.

I never crossed his door
   But still preferred
To hunt some orchid or
   Watch for a bird.

We went one day to church,
   His friends and he;
We left him in the lurch,
   As it seemed to me.

But still from his grave he says,
   'You know the house;
You must one of these days
   Drop in on us.'

Mist

Rain, do not fall
Nor rob this mist at all,
That is my only cell and abbey wall.

Wind, wait to blow
And let the thick mist grow,
That fills the rose-cup with a whiter glow.

Mist, deepen still
And the low valley fill;
You hide but taller trees, a higher hill.

Still, mist, draw close;
These gain by what they lose,
The taller trees and hill, the whiter rose.

All else begone,
And leave me here alone
To tread this mist where earth and sky are one.

Penelope

The leaves hang on the boughs
Filemot, ochreous,
Or fall and strangely greet
Green blades of winter wheat.
The long buds of the beech
Point where they cannot reach.

A sad Telemachus,
I stand under the boughs;
Patient Penelope,
Her heart across the sea,
Another year unweaves
Her web of wasted leaves.

Is bud and leaf and flower
All we are waiting for?
But we shall wait again
When these are gone, and then
When they are gone and gone
Penelope alone.

The Wood

Summer's green tide rises in flood
Foaming with elder-blossom in the wood,
And insects hawk, gold-striped and blue,
On motion-hidden wings the air looks through,
And 'Buzz, buzz, buzz',
Gaily hums Sir Pandarus,
As blue ground-ivy blossom
Bends with the weight of a bee in its bosom.

Heavy with leaves the boughs lean over
The path where midges in a loose ball hover,
And daisies and slow-footed moss
And thin grass creep across,
Till scarcely on the narrow path
The sparrow finds a dusty bath,
And caterpillars from the leaves
Arch their green backs on my coat-sleeves.

Bright as a bird the small sun flits
Through shaking leaves that tear the sky in bits;
But let the leaf-lit boughs draw closer,
I in the dark will feel no loser
With myself for companion.
Grow, leafy boughs; darken, O sun,
For here two robins mate
That winter held apart in a cold hate.

The Signpost

Snowflakes dance on the night;
   A single star
Glows with a wide blue light
   On Lochnagar.

Through snow-fields trails the Dee;
   At the wind's breath
An ermine-clad spruce-tree
   Spits snow beneath.

White-armed at the roadside
   Wails a signpost,
'Tonight the world has died
   And left its ghost.'

The Rain

Fair mornings make false vows!
   When to that wood I came
I stood beneath fast-dripping boughs
   And watched the green leaves wink
   Spilling their heavy drink;
Some flowers to sleeping buds returned,
Some, lit by rain, with clear flames burned;
'Cuckoo' – again, again
   A cuckoo called his name
Behind the waving veil of dismal rain.

The rain bit yellow root
   And shone on the blue flints
And dangled like a silver fruit
   From blackened twigs and boughs;
   I watched those running rows
Splash on the sodden earth and wet
The empty snail-shells marked 'To let',
And whitened worms that lay
   Like stalks of hyacinths,
The last end of a children's holiday.

I heard a dead man cough
   Not twenty yards away –
(A wool-wet sheep, likely enough,
   As I thought afterwards);
   But O those shrieking birds!
   And how the flowers seemed to outstare
Some hidden sun in that dim air,
As sadly the rain soaked
   To where the dead man lay
Whose cough a sudden fall of earth had choked.

Palmistry

I lifted from the ground my grass-pressed hand
And pondered, as its strange new lines I scanned,
What is foretold? What hope, what fear,
What strife, what passion is prefigured here?

The Feather

Briar, spindle and thorn tangled together
    Made dark the narrow track,
And from some hoarse-voiced rook the fallen feather
    That lay silent and black.

Gold lees left in the pink cup of dog-roses
    Nor the red campion
That the June cuckoo when his voice he loses
    Casts his white spittle on,

Nothing could lighten that track's narrow gloom,
    Except on ground or bark
Some honied light straggling through branches from
    The sun that made it dark.

The White Blackbird
(1935)

The Loddon

Through hoof-marked meadows that lie sodden
From winter's overflow, the Loddon
Winds by the winding pollard hedge, –
Stunt willow-trunks that line the edge,
Whose roots like buried eels are sunk,
A grove of saplings on each trunk.

Its water with a white-frothed mouth
Chewing and gnawing the uncouth
Loose sticks and straws that in disorder
Lie littered on its leaping border,
As breath of wind roughens its hide,
This way or that way makes its tide.

This way or that – But O let come
May-blossom that in buds lies dumb,
This water that laps bush and tree
Shall long have drifted to the sea;
I almost feel that I too go
Caught in its secret lapsing flow.

The Knotted Ash

Is this a lover's vow?
Who else should tie it and for what,
This olive-coloured sapling in a knot,
Till now spring's sap must stoop
And bend back in a gouty loop
Rising from root to sooty-budded bough?

They may be tired of love,
Who found it not enough
To twine the glances of their eyes
Like kissing brimstone butterflies;
But death itself can not untwist
This piteous tree-contortionist.

The Bird

The blackbird darted through the boughs
Trailing his whistle in a shrill dispute
'Why do you loiter near our house?'
But I was mute,
Though as he perched with sidelong head
I might have said,
'I never notice nests or lovers
In hedges or in covers;
I have enough to do
In my own way to be unnoticed too.'

Stay, Spring

Stay, spring, for by this ruthless haste
You turn all good to waste;
Look, how the blackthorn now
Changes to trifling dust upon the bough.

Where blossom from the wild pear shakes
Too rare a china breaks,
And though the cuckoos shout
They will forget their name ere June is out.

That thrush too, that with beadlike eye
Watches each passer-by,
Is warming at her breast
A brood that when they fly rob their own nest.

So late begun, so early ended!
Lest I should be offended
Take warning, spring, and stay
Or I might never turn to look your way.

Sea Wormwood

It grew about my feet
Like frost unmelted in the summer heat;
I plucked it and such oozes
Flowed from its broken bruises
That as I turned inland
Its loosened scent was hanging from my hand.

And so I thought the people
Stayed from pea-picking by the road to Steeple,
No, not to watch the stranger
Who landed from Goldhanger,
But breathe the odorous oil
That flowing from his hand sweetened their toil.

Black Rock of Kiltearn

They named it Aultgraat – Ugly Burn,
This water through the crevice hurled
Scouring the entrails of the world –
Not ugly in the rising smoke
That clothes it with a rainbowed cloak.
But slip a foot on frost-spiked stone
Above this rock-lipped Phlegethon
And you shall have
The Black Rock of Kiltearn
For tombstone, grave
And trumpet of your resurrection.

The Eagle

He hangs between his wings outspread
   Level and still
And bends a narrow golden head,
   Scanning the ground to kill.

Yet as he sails and smoothly swings
   Round the hillside,
He looks as though from his own wings
   He hung down crucified.

The Ruined Chapel

From meadows with the sheep so shorn
They, not their lambs, seem newly born
Through the graveyard I pass,
Where only blue plume-thistle waves
And headstones lie so deep in grass
They follow dead men to their graves,
And as I enter by no door
This chapel where the slow moss crawls
I wonder that so small a floor
Can have the sky for roof, mountains for walls.

The Fairy Ring

Here the horse-mushrooms make a fairy ring,
    Some standing upright and some overthrown,
A small Stonehenge, where heavy black snails cling
    And bite away, like Time, the tender stone.

The Slow Race

I followed each detour
Of the slow meadow-winding Stour,
That looked on cloud, tree, hill,
And mostly flowed by standing still.

Fearing to go too quick
I stopped at time to throw a stick
Or see how in the copse
The last snow was the first snowdrops.

The river also tarried
So much of sky and earth it carried,
Or even changed its mind
To flow back with a flaw of wind.

And when we reached the weir
That combed the water's silver hair,
I knew I lost the race –
I could not keep so slow a pace.

Young Oats

These oats in autumn sown,
That stood through all the winter's dearth
In so small ranks of green
That flints like pigmies' bones lay bare
And greater stones were seen
To change to hares and rise and run,
Today to such a height are grown
That drawn up by the sun,
That Indian conjuror,
The field is levitated from the earth.

Gossip

The wind shaking the gate
Impatiently as though in haste and late
Shook and shook it making it rattle,
And all the other tittle-tattle
It rushed to tell, –
Of how mahogany chestnuts fell
And how the gamekeeper
Had crackling paper here and there and there
To frighten pheasants back into the wood,
And how the flapping scarecrow stood
And guarding seeds from harm
Saluted with a broken arm,
And how the thin-voiced lamb
Still in the autumn sucked his dam,
A late and casual love-begot,
All that I heard and proudly thought
That I, a man, whom most things hate,
Shared country gossip with the wind and gate.

An Evening Walk

I never saw a lovelier sky;
The faces of the passers-by
Shine with gold light as they step west
As though by secret joy possessed,
Some rapture that is not of earth
But in that heavenly climate has its birth.

I know it is the sunlight paints
The faces of these travelling saints,
But shall I hold in cold misprision
The calm and beauty of that vision
Upturned a moment from the sorrow
That makes today today, tomorrow tomorrow?

Mole-hills on the Downs

Here earth in her abundance spills
Hills on her hills,
Till every hill is overgrown
With small hills of its own;
Some old with moss and scorpion-grass,
Some new and bare and brown,
And one where I can watch the earth
Like a volcano at its birth
Still rise by falling down;
And as by these small hills I pass
And take them in my stride
I swell with pride,
Till the great hills to which I lift my eyes
Restore my size.

The Tree

Tree, lend me this root,
That I may sit here at your foot
And watch these hawking flies that wheel
And perch on the air's hand
And red-thighed bees
That fan the dust with their wings' breeze.
Do you not feel me on your heel,
My bone against your bone?
Or are you in such slumber sunk,
Woodpeckers knocking at your trunk
Find you are not at home?
To winds you are not dumb;
Then tell me, if you understand:
When your thick timber has been hewn,
Its boards in floors and fences sewn,
And you no more a tree,
Where will your dryad be?

The Sunbeams

The tired road climbed the hill
Through trees with light-spots never still,
Gold mouths that drew apart and singled
And ran again and met and mingled,
Two, three or five or seven,
No other way than souls that love in heaven.

Sunny and swift and cool
They danced there like Bethesda's pool;
Ah, if in those pale kissing suns
My halting feet could bathe but once
No slender stick would crack,
My footstep falling on its brittle back.

In Teesdale

No, not tonight,
Not by this fading light,
Not by those high fells where the forces
Fall from the mist like the white tails of horses.

From that dark slack
Where peat-hags gape too black
I turn to where the lighted farm
Holds out through the open door a golden arm.

No, not tonight,
Tomorrow by daylight;
Tonight I fear the fabulous horses
Whose white tails flash down the steep water-courses.

A Windy Day

This wind brings all dead things to life,
Branches that lash the air like whips
And dead leaves rolling in a hurry
Or peering in a rabbits' bury
Or trying to push down a tree;
Gates that fly open to the wind
And close again behind,
And fields that are a flowing sea
And make the cattle look like ships;
Straws glistening and stiff
Lying on air as on a shelf
And pond that leaps to leave itself;
And feathers too that rise and float,
Each feather changed into a bird,
And line-hung sheets that crack and strain;
Even the sun-greened coat,
That through so many winds has served,
The scarecrow struggles to put on again.

The Dead Crab

A rosy shield upon its back,
That not the hardest storm could crack,
From whose sharp edge projected out
Black pinpoint eyes staring about;
Beneath, the well-knit cote-armure
That gave to its weak belly power;
The clustered legs with plated joints
That ended in stiletto points;
The claws like mouths it held outside: –
I cannot think this creature died
By storm or fish or sea-fowl harmed
Walking the sea so heavily armed;
Or does it make for death to be
Oneself a living armoury?

To the River Dove

Swift under hollow shelf
Or spreading out to rest yourself
You flow between high ridge and ridge
To brim the heavy eyebrows of the bridge.

No, Dove, it is not mine
To stroke you with a fly and line,
A legless trunk wading your water;
I leave your fish to heron, pike and otter,

And him who haunts that inn
With 'Isaac Walton' for its sign,
Living there still as he lived once,
A wind-blown picture now, with creaking bones.

The Dark Wood

O wood, now you are dark with summer
Your birds grow dumber
And ink-stained leaves of sycamore
Slide slowly down and hit your floor;
But there are other signs I mark,
In ivy with the sunlight wet
And dried rains streaming down your bark,
A withered limb, a broken shoulder,
Signs that since first we met
Even you, O wood, have grown a little older.

On Middleton Edge

If this life-saving rock should fail
Yielding too much to my embrace
And rock and I to death should race,
The rock would stay there in the dale
While I, breaking my fall,
Would still go on
Farther than any wandering star has gone.

The Swans

How lovely are these swans,
That float like high proud galleons
Cool in the summer heat,
And waving leaf-like feet
Divide with narrow breasts of snow
In a smooth surge
This water that is mostly sky;
So lovely that I know
Death cannot kill such birds,
It could but wound them, mortally.

The Stones

Though the thick glacier,
That filled the mountains' rocky jaws
And lifted these great rocks like straws
And dropped them here,
Has shrunk to this small ale-brown burn,
Where trout like shadows dart and turn,
The stones in awkward stance
Still wait some starry circumstance
To bring the ice once more
And bear them to a distant shore.

The White Blackbird

Gulls that in meadows stand,
The sea their native land,
Are not so white as you
Flitting from bough to bough,
You who are white as sin
To your black kith and kin.

The Copse

Here in the Horseshoe Copse
The may in such a snow-storm drops
That every stick and stone
Becomes a tree with blossom of its own.

And though loose sun-spots sway
The night so lasts through all the day
That no bird great or small
Sings in these trees but is a nightingale.

Time might be anything,
Morning or night, winter or spring;
One who in this copse strays
Must walk through many months of night and days.

The Cuckoo

This year the leaves were late and thin,
And my eye wandering softly in
Saw perched upon a topmost twig,
Small bird to have a voice so big,
A cuckoo with long tail behind,
Twig and bird aswing on the wind,
That rose and flew with outspread tail
Guiding his flight like steering sail.

I waited, listened; came again
Across the distance of the rain
'Cuckoo' so faint and far away
It sounded out of yesterday,
Making me start with sudden fear
Lest spring that had seemed new and near
Was gone already. A sparrow hopped
In white plum-tree and blossom dropped.

Eryngo

I came on that blue-headed plant
    That lovers ate to waken love,
Eryngo; but I felt no want,
    A lovesick swain, to eat thereof.

Wood and Hill

Nowhere is one alone
And in the closest covert least,
But to small eye of bird or beast
He will be known;
Today it was for me
A squirrel that embraced a tree
Turning a small head round;
A hare too that ran up the hill,
To his short forelegs level ground,
And with tall ears stood still.
But it was birds I could not see
And larks that tried to stand on air
That made of wood and hill a market-square.

The Fallen Tree

The shade once swept about your boughs
Quietly obsequious
To the time-keeping sun;
Now, fallen tree, you with that shade are one.

From chalky earth as white as surf
Beneath the uptorn turf
Roots hang in empty space
Like snakes about the pale Medusa's face.

And as I perch on a forked branch,
More used to squirrel's haunch,
I think how dead you are,
More dead than upright post or fence or chair.

By the Tyne

What foolish birds were they
That built these nests exposed to day,
A score on every tree
So darkly clear between the river and me?

Not birds that haunt these woods,
But heavy, hurrying winter floods
With their foam-hissing billows
Left these wild driftwood nests on the lean willows.

The Fear

How often I turn round
To face the beast that bound by bound
Leaps on me from behind,
Only to see a bough that heaves
With sudden gust of wind
Or blackbird raking withered leaves.

A dog may find me out
Or badger toss a white-lined snout;
And one day as I softly trod
Looking for nothing stranger than
A fox or stoat I met a man
And even that seemed not too odd.

And yet in any place I go
I watch and listen as all creatures do
For what I cannot see or hear,
For something warns me everywhere
That even in my land of birth
I trespass on the earth.

The Stockdoves

They rose up in a twinkling cloud
And wheeled about and bowed
To settle on the trees
Perching like small clay images.

Then with a noise of sudden rain
They clattered off again
And over Ballard Down
They circled like a flying town.

Though one could sooner blast a rock
Than scatter that dense flock
That through the winter weather
Some iron rule has held together,

Yet in another month from now
Love like a spark will blow
Those birds the country over
To drop in trees, lover by lover.

The Secret Wood

Where there is nothing more to see
Than this old earth-bound tree
That years ago dry sawdust bled
But sprouts each spring a leaf or two
As though it tried not to be dead,
Or that down-hanging broken bough
That keeps its withered leaves till now,
Like a dead man that cannot move
Or take his own clothes off,
What is it that I seek or who,
Fearing from passer-by
Intrusion of a foot or eye?
I only know
Though all men of earth's beauty speak
Beauty here I do not seek
More than I sought it on my mother's cheek.

A Heap of Faggots

Faggots of ash, elm, oak
That dark loose snowflakes touch and soak,
An unlit fire they lie
With cold inhospitality.

Nothing will light them now,
Sticks that with only lichen glow
And crumble to touchwood
Soft and unfit for fire's food.

And with wren, finch and tit
And all the silent birds that sit
In this snow-travelled wood
I warm myself at my own blood.

57

Ploughing in the Mist

Pulling the shoulder-sack
Closer about his neck and back,
He called out to his team
That stamped off dragging the weigh-beam;
And as he gripped the stilts and steered
They plunged in mist and disappeared,
Fading so fast away
They seemed on a long journey gone,
Not to return that day;
But while I waited on
The jingle of loose links I caught,
And suddenly on the hill-rise,
Pale phantoms of the mist at first,
Man and his horses burst
As though before my eyes
Creation had been wrought.

The Comet

Why do I idly stand
And digging with my finger-tips
Tear the tree-trunk in strips?
Because such touchwood soft and damp
I once would stuff in a clay lamp
And blow on it with fiery face
To coax a sparkling light
And through the darkness race,
That lit lamp in my hand
A comet streaming through the autumn night.

Autumn

A new Teiresias and unreproved,
Not stricken by the goddess that I loved,
Today I looked and saw the earth undress
With intimate and godlike carelessness.

In the Fallow Field

I went down on my hands and knees
Looking for trees,
Twin leaves that, sprung from seeds,
Were now too big
For stems much thinner than a twig.
These soon with chamomile and clover
And other fallow weeds
Would be turned over;
And I was thinking how
It was a pity someone should not know
That a great forest fell before the plough.

The Paps of Jura

Before I crossed the sound
   I saw how from the sea
These breasts rise soft and round,
    Not two but three;

Now, climbing, I clasp rocks
   Storm-shattered and sharp-edged,
Grey ptarmigan their flocks,
    With starved moss wedged;

And mist like hair hangs over
   One barren breast and me,
Who climb, a desperate lover,
    With hand and knee.

Fenland

Where sky is all around
And creeps in dykes along the ground,
I see trees stand outlined
Too distant to be tossed with wind.

And farther still than these
Stand but the tops of other trees,
As on the ocean's rim
Vessels half-sunk in water swim.

Where there is so much sky
And earth so level to my eye,
Trees and trees farther hide
Far down the steep world's mountain-side.

Last Snow

Although the snow still lingers
Heaped on the ivy's blunt webbed fingers
And painting tree-trunks on one side,
Here in this sunlit ride
The fresh unchristened things appear,
Leaf, spathe and stem,
With crumbs of earth clinging to them
To show the way they came
But no flower yet to tell their name,
And one green spear
Stabbing a dead leaf from below
Kills winter at a blow.

The Track

Trodden by man and horse
Tracks change their course
As rivers change their bed;
And this that I now tread,
Where the lean roots obtrude,
Was not the first track through the wood.

There older traces flow,
Where ghosts may go
But no one else save I;
And as in turn I try
Each faint and fainter track,
Through what long ages I fall back.

Thistledown

Silver against blue sky
These ghosts of day float by,
Fitful, irregular,
Each one a silk-haired star,
Till from the wind's aid freed
They settle on their seed.

Not by the famished light
Of a moon-ridden night
But by clear sunny hours
Gaily these ghosts of flowers
With rise and swirl and fall
Dance to their burial.

New Poems

(in *Collected Poems*, 1936)

The Chalk-Cliff

Blasted and bored and undermined
   By quarrying seas
Reared the erect chalk-cliff with black flints lined.
   (Flints drop like nuts from trees
When the frost bites
The chalk on winter nights.)

Save for frail shade of jackdaw's flight
   No night was there,
But blue-skyed summer and a cliff so white
   It stood like frozen air;
Foot slipped on damp
Chalk where the limpets camp.

With only purple of sea-stock
   And jackdaw's shade
To mitigate that blazing height of chalk
   I stood like a soul strayed
In paradise
Hiding my blinded eyes.

The Elm-Beetle

So long I sat and conned
That naked bole
With the strange hieroglyphics scored
That those small priests,
The beetle-grubs, had bored,
Telling of gods and kings and beasts
And the long journey of the soul
Through magic-opened gates
To where the throned Osiris waits,
That when at last I woke
I stepped from an Egyptian tomb
To see the wood's sun-spotted gloom,
And rising cottage smoke
That leaned upon the wind and broke,
Roller-striped fields, and smooth cow-shadowed pond.

The Missel-Thrush

That missel-thrush
Scorns to alight on a low bush,
And as he flies
And tree-top after tree-top tries,
His shadow flits
And harmlessly on tree-trunk hits.

Shutting his wings
He sways and sings and sways and sings,
And from his bough
As in deep water he looks through
He sees me there
Crawl at the bottom of the air.

Cuckoo in May

Cuckoo that like a cuckoo-clock
Calls out the hours so fast,
Days, months and years go slipping past,
O for a while be dumb
Lest in a moment I become
Old as that man I stopped to watch
And chat with in my morning walk,
His back as rounded as a hoop,
Who did not need to stoop
To pull out weeds in his potato-patch.

August

The cows stood in a thundercloud of flies,
   As lagging through the field with trailing feet
I kicked up scores of skipper butterflies
   That hopped a little way, lazy with heat.

The wood I found was in deep shelter sunk,
   Though bryony leaves shone with a glossy sweat
And creeping over ground and up tree-trunk
   The ivy in the sun gleamed bright and wet.

Songs brief as Chinese poems the birds sung
   And insects of all sheens, blue, brown and yellow,
Darted and twisted in their flight and hung
   On air that groaned like hoarse sweet violoncello.

No leaf stirred in the wood-discouraged wind,
   But foliage hung on trees like heavy wigs;
The sun, come from the sky, was close behind
   The fire-fringed leaves and in among the twigs.

The Scarecrow

He strides across the grassy corn
That has not grown since it was born,
A piece of sacking on a pole,
A ghost, but nothing like a soul.

Why must this dead man haunt the spring
With arms anxiously beckoning?
Is spring not hard enough to bear
For one at autumn of his year?

The Nest

Four blue stones in this thrush's nest
I leave, content to make the best
Of turquoise, lapis lazuli
Or for that matter of the whole blue sky.

February

So thick a mist darkened the day
Not two trees distant flew my friend, the jay,
　　To keep love's angry tryst
　　Somewhere in the damp mist,
　　And as I brushed each bush
　　Rain-buds fell in a rush,
One might have said it rained,
While green buds on the barer boughs remained.

But where with looped and twisted twine
Wild clematis, bryony and woodbine
　　And such reptilian growth
　　Hung in decaying sloth,
　　I stood still thinking how
　　Two months or three from now
The green buds would not tarry
More than those flashing drops of February.

Autumn Seeds

Although a thoughtful bee still travels
And midge-ball ravels and unravels,
Yet strewn along the pathway lie
Like small open sarcophagi
The hazel-nuts broken in two
And cobwebs catch the seed-pearl dew.

Now summer's flowers are winter's weeds,
I think of all the sleeping seeds;
Winds were their robins and by night
Frosts glue their leafy cover tight;
Snow may shake down its dizzy feathers,
They will sleep safely through all weathers.

The Ventriloquists

The birds sang in the rain
    That rhythmically waving its grey veil
From smoking hilltop flowed to misty plain,
    Where one white house shone sharply as a sail;

But not so bright as these,
    The anemones that held the wood snow-bound,
The water-drops waiting to fall from trees,
    The rusty catkins crawling on the ground.

March buds give little shelter;
    Better seek shelter in the open rain
Than where tree-gathered showers fall helter-skelter,
    I meditated; but 'Turn, turn again',

The birds shrieked through their song;
    So rooted to the leaf-soft earth I stood,
Letting my restless eye wander among
    The thick sky-crawling branches of the wood.

But no bird could I see
    In criss-cross of thin twigs or sudden twists
Where branching tree interrupted branching tree;
    Yet everywhere those hidden ventriloquists

Were singing in the wood,
    Flinging their cheating voices here and there;
But seeing nothing though I walked or stood
    I thought the singing grew out of the air.

The Echoing Cliff

White gulls that sit and float,
Each on his shadow like a boat,
Sandpipers, oystercatchers
And herons, those grey stilted watchers,
From loch and corran rise,
And as they scream and squawk abuse
Echo from wooded cliff replies
So clearly that the dark pine boughs,
Where goldcrests flit
And owls in drowsy wisdom sit,
Are filled with sea-birds and their cries.

South Downs

No water cries among these hills,
   The mist hides and enlarges,
Though rain in every road-rut spills
   Where leaves have sunk their barges.

No freshet in a hollow brake
   Utters its shy cold fears,
Only the chiming sheep-bells make
   One Sabbath of the years.

Walking in Beech Leaves

I tread on many autumns here
   But with no pride,
For at the leaf-fall of each year
   I also died.

This is last autumn, crisp and brown,
   That my knees feel;
But through how many years sinks down
   My sullen heel.

Man and Cows

I stood aside to let the cows
Swing past me with their wrinkled brows,
Bowing their heads as they went by
As to a woodland deity
To whom they turned mute eyes
To save them from the plaguing god of flies.

And I too cursed Beelzebub,
Watching them stop to rub
A bulging side or bony haunch
Against a trunk or pointing branch
And lift a tufted tail
To thresh the air with its soft flail.

They stumbled heavily down the slope,
As Hathor led them or the hope
Of the lush meadow-grass,
While I remained, thinking it was
Strange that we both were held divine,
In Egypt these, man once in Palestine.

The Mountain

The burn ran blacker for the snow
And ice-floe on ice-floe
Jangled in heavy lurches
Beneath the claret-coloured birches.

Dark grouse rose becking from the ground
And deer turned sharp heads round,
The antlers on their brows
Like stunted trees with withered boughs.

I climbed to where the mountain sloped
And long wan bubbles groped
Under the ice's cover,
A bridge that groaned as I crossed over.

I reached the mist, brighter than day,
That showed a specious way
By narrow crumbling shelves,
Where rocks grew larger than themselves.

But when I saw the mountain's spire
Looming through that damp fire,
I left it still unwon
And climbed down to the setting sun.

The Chalk-Quarry

A solitary yew,
    Fern-haired and ruddy-thewed,
That light with no sharp needle can prick through,
    Itself makes a small forest in the wood.

The strong sun darkening still
    That yew's *memento mori*
Fills with a fiercer light out on the hill
    The open sepulchre of the old chalk-quarry.

Snow

Ridged thickly on black bough
    And foaming on twig-fork in swollen lumps
At flirt of bird-wing or wind's sough
    Plump snow tumbled on snow softly with sudden dumps.

Where early steps had made
    A wavering track through the white-blotted road
Breaking its brightness with blue shade,
    Snow creaked beneath my feet with snow heavily shod.

I reached a snow-thatched rick
    Where men sawed bedding off for horse and cow;
There varnished straws were lying thick
    Paving with streaky gold the trodden silver snow.

Such light filled me with awe
    And nothing marred my paradisal thought,
That robin least of all I saw
    Lying too fast asleep, his song choked in his throat.

Speak to the Earth
(1939)

Culbin Sands

Here lay a fair fat land;
   But now its townships, kirks, graveyards
Beneath bald hills of sand
   Lie buried deep as Babylonian shards.

But gales may blow again;
   And like a sand-glass turned about
The hills in a dry rain
   Will flow away and the old land look out;

And where now hedgehog delves
   And conies hollow their long caves
Houses will build themselves
   And tombstones rewrite names on dead men's graves.

Glow-Worms

As though the dark had called
To chrysolite and emerald,
Earth brings out jewel by jewel,
Love stoking their bright fires, itself the fuel.

To flying beetles, 'Come,
Find here your children and your home,'
They sing with a green light,
Each glow-worm her own Venus in the night.

Autumn Mist

So thick a mist hung over all,
Rain had no room to fall;
It seemed a sea without a shore;
The cobwebs drooped heavy and hoar
As though with wool they had been knit;
Too obvious mark for fly to hit!

And though the sun was somewhere else
The gloom had brightness of its own
That shone on bracken, grass and stone
And mole-mound with its broken shells
That told where squirrel lately sat,
Cracked hazel-nuts and ate the fat.

And sullen haws in the hedgerows
Burned in the damp with clearer fire;
And brighter still than those
The scarlet hips hung on the briar
Like coffins of the dead dog-rose;
All were as bright as though for earth
Death were a gayer thing than birth.

A Dead Mole

Strong-shouldered mole,
That so much lived below the ground,
Dug, fought and loved, hunted and fed,
For you to raise a mound
Was as for us to make a hole;
What wonder now that being dead
Your body lies here stout and square
Buried within the blue vault of the air?

Children Gathering Violets

Children, small Herods, slay these Innocents
With blue untidy faces and sweet scents;
But violets gone or even autumn here
Spring in the children lasts through all the year.

Wiltshire Downs

The cuckoo's double note
Loosened like bubbles from a drowning throat
Floats through the air
In mockery of pipit, lark and stare.

The stable-boys thud by
Their horses slinging divots at the sky
And with bright hooves
Printing the sodden turf with lucky grooves.

As still as a windhover
A shepherd in his flapping coat leans over
His tall sheep-crook
And shearlings, tegs and yoes cons like a book.

And one tree-crowned long barrow
Stretched like a sow that has brought forth her farrow
Hides a king's bones
Lying like broken sticks among the stones.

Suilven

It rose dark as a stack of peat
With mountains at its feet,
Till a bright flush of evening swept
And on to its high shoulders leapt
And Suilven, a great ruby, shone;
And though that evening light is dead,
The mountain in my mind burns on,
As though I were the foul toad, said
To bear a precious jewel in his head.

Mountain View

Can those small hills lying below
Be mountains that some hours ago
I gazed at from beneath?
Can such intense blue be the sea's
Or that long cloud the Hebrides?
Perhaps I prayed enough
By crawling up on hands and knees
The sharp loose screes,
Sweat dripping on the lichen's scurf,
And now in answer to my prayer
A vision is laid bare;
Or on that ledge, holding my breath,
I may have even slipped past Death.

Snow Harvest

The moon that now and then last night
Glanced between clouds in flight
Saw the white harvest that spread over
The stubble fields and even roots and clover.

It climbed the hedges, overflowed
And trespassed on the road,
Weighed down fruit-trees and when winds woke
From white-thatched roofs rose in a silver smoke.

How busy is the world today!
Sun reaps, rills bear away
The lovely harvest of the snow
While bushes weep loud tears to see it go.

Cuckoos

When coltsfoot withers and begins to wear
Long silver locks instead of golden hair,
And fat red catkins from black poplars fall
And on the ground like caterpillars crawl,
And bracken lifts up slender arms and wrists
And stretches them, unfolding sleepy fists,
The cuckoos in a few well-chosen words
Tell they give Easter eggs to the small birds.

The Shepherd's Hut

Now when I could not find the road
Unless beside it also flowed
This cobbled beck that through the night,
Breaking on stones, makes its own light,

Where blackness in the starlit sky
Is all I know a mountain by,
A shepherd little thinks how far
His lamp is shining like a star.

A Brimstone Butterfly

The autumn sun that rose at seven
Has risen again at noon,
Where the hill makes a later heaven,
And fringing with bright rainbow hair
The boughs that lace the sky
Has wakened half a year too soon
This brimstone butterfly,
That fluttering every way at once
Searches in vain the moss and stones, –
Itself the only primrose there.

Drought in the Fens

How often from the shade of trees
I thought of that rich man, Dives,
And how no diamond drop was given
To his or earth's cracked lips from heaven.

Green apples fell and lay around
As though they grew upon the ground,
And ditches, shrunk to muddy roads,
Starved limbless fish and man-legged toads.

So when the sand-walled flats I crossed
Hardened by heat as by a frost,
How strange it was that there could be
Still so much water in the sea.

The Gramophone

We listened to your birds tonight
By the firelight,
The nightingales that trilled to us
From moonlit boughs.

Though golden snowflakes from the gloom
Looked in the room,
Those birds' clear voices lingered on
Your gramophone.

'Goodnight' we said and as I go
High-heeled with snow
I almost hope to hear one now
From a bare bough.

A Prehistoric Camp

It was the time of year
    Pale lambs leap with thick leggings on
Over small hills that are not there,
    That I climbed Eggardon.

The hedgerows still were bare,
    None ever knew so late a year;
Birds built their nests in the open air,
    Love conquering their fear.

But there on the hill-crest,
    Where only larks or stars look down,
Earthworks exposed a vaster nest,
    Its race of men long flown.

The Swallows

All day – when early morning shone
With every dewdrop its own dawn
And when cockchafers were abroad
Hurtling like missiles that had lost their road –

The swallows twisting here and there
Round unseen corners of the air
Upstream and down so quickly passed
I wondered that their shadows flew as fast.

They steeplechased over the bridge
And dropped down to a drowning midge
Sharing the river with the fish,
Although the air itself was their chief dish.

Blue-winged snowballs! until they turned
And then with ruddy breasts they burned;
All in one instant everywhere,
Jugglers with their own bodies in the air.

A Wet Day

Breasting the thick brushwood that hid my track
Diffuse wetness of rain had stained me black;
My clinging coat I hung on a bough-knop
And sodden shapeless hat I laid on top.

With heavy hat and coat left on the bough
I felt a snake that had cast off his slough
And joined the slow black slugs that strolled abroad
Making soft shameless love on the open road.

But, turning on my steps, startled I stood
To see a dead man hanging in the wood;
By two clear feet of air he swung afloat,
One who had hanged himself in hat and coat.

Nightfall on Sedgemoor

The darkness like a guillotine
    Descends on the flat earth;
The flocks look white across the rhine
    All but one lamb, a negro from its birth.

The pollards hold up in the gloom
    Knobbed heads with long stiff hair
That the wind tries to make a broom
    To sweep the moon's faint feather from the air.

What makes the darkness fall so soon
    Is not the short March day
Nor the white sheep nor brightening moon,
    But long June evenings when I came this way.

Reflections on the River

Rose-petals fall without a touch
As though it were too much
I should be standing by,
And poplars in no wind at all
Keep swaying left and right
With the slow motion of their height
Beneath a small white cloud that soon
Will pluck light from the dark and be the moon.

But where roach rise and bite the Ouse
Round ripples spread out like the first
Drops of a storm about to burst
And in the water toss the boughs
And crack the garden wall;
And as I gaze down in the sky
I see the whole vault shake
As though the heavens were seized with an earthquake.

Passing the Graveyard

I see you did not try to save
The bouquet of white flowers I gave;
So fast they wither on your grave.

Why does it hurt the heart to think
Of that most bitter abrupt brink
Where the low-shouldered coffins sink?

These living bodies that we wear
So change by every seventh year
That in a new dress we appear;

Limbs, spongy brain and slogging heart,
No part remains the selfsame part;
Like streams they stay and still depart.

You slipped slow bodies in the past;
Then why should we be so aghast
You flung off the whole flesh at last?

Let him who loves you think instead
That like a woman who has wed
You undressed first and went to bed.

Walking in Mist

At first the river Noe
Like a snake's belly gleamed below,
And then in mist was lost;
The hill too vanished like a ghost
And all the day was gone
Except the damp grey light that round me shone.

From Lose Hill to Mam Tor,
Darkness behind me and before,
I gave the track its head;
But as I followed where it led,
That light went all the way
As though I made and carried my own day.

Climbing in Glencoe

The sun became a small round moon
And the scared rocks grew pale and weak
As mist surged up the col, and soon
So thickly everywhere it tossed
That though I reached the peak
With height and depth both lost
It might as well have been a plain;
Yet when, groping my way again,
On to the scree I stept
It went with me, and as I swept
Down its loose rumbling course
Balanced I rode it like a circus horse.

The Thunderstorm

When Coniston Old Man was younger
And his deep-quarried sides were stronger,
Goats may have leapt about Goat's Water;
But why the tarn that looks like its young daughter
Though lying high under the fell
Should be called Blind Tarn, who can tell?

For from Dow Crag, passing it by,
I saw it as a dark presageful eye;
And soon I knew that I was not mistaken
Hearing the thunder the loose echoes waken
About Scafell and Scafell Pike
And feeling the slant raindrops strike.

And when I came to Walna Pass
Hailstones hissing and hopping among the grass,
Beneath a rock I found a hole;
But with sharp crack and rumbling roll on roll
So quick the lightning came and went
The solid rock was like a lighted tent.

Fields of Asparagus

From their long narrow beds
Asparagus raise reptilian heads
(Even the sand in May awakes)
And men who think that they are snakes
With shining knives
Walk to and fro, taking their scaly lives.

My path goes to the sea
But turning round comes back to me
In clouds of wind-blown sand
Making a desert of the land,
Where men must fight
With purple snakes that grow up in a night.

After the Gale

I pity trees that all their life
Have ivy for a wife
Or with dark mistletoe they bear
Keep Christmas through the year.

So seeing oak-twigs grow on thorn
Where they were never born,
And sprays of ash-keys and pine-cones
Grow on a briar at once,

I blamed the gale that through the night
Had with perverse delight
Quartered rich children on the poor
Like foundlings at their door.

Idleness

God, you've so much to do,
To think of, watch and listen to,
That I will let all else go by
And lending ear and eye
Help you to watch how in the combe
Winds sweep dead leaves without a broom;
And rooks in the spring-reddened trees
Restore their villages,
Nest by dark nest
Swaying at rest on the trees' frail unrest;
Or on this limestone wall,
Leaning at ease, with you recall
How once these heavy stones
Swam in the sea as shells and bones;
And hear that owl snore in a tree
Till it grows dark enough for him to see;
In fact, will learn to shirk
No idleness that I may share your work.

The Falls of Glomach

Rain drifts forever in this place
Tossed from the long white lace
The Falls trail on black rocks below,
And golden-rod and rose-root shake
In wind that they forever make;
So though they wear their own rainbow
It's not in hope, but just for show,
For rain and wind together
Here through the summer make a chill wet weather.

The Frogs

Each night that I come down the strath
Frogs turn heels-over-head,
And their white bellies on the path
Tell where to tread.

Of fox with brush above the brake
And kestrel pinned to air
And thin dark river of a snake
Let them beware!

Fat acrobats, I watch them turn
Kicking the evening dew,
Till in white waves that ride the burn
I see frogs too.

Long Meg and her Daughters

When from the Druid's Head I came
The low sun doubled tussock-tump
And half in shadow, half in flame
Stood the Stone Circle. Lump by lump
Viewing her daughters Long Meg said,
'Come, stranger, make your choice of one;
All are my children, stone of my stone,
And none of them yet wed;
They wait to play at kiss-in-the-ring
With only now the wind to sing.'
But I, 'No, mother, all are fat
And some too old have fallen down flat.'
Meg frowned, 'You should be dead
To take instead a young tombstone to bed.'

Ba Cottage

There at the watershed I turned
And looked back at the house I burned –
Burnt, too, by many another tramp
Who sought its shelter, dry or damp.

For coming from the mist-thick moor
I made the window-sill my door
And, wet incendiary, tore up wood
And fed the grate's wide mouth with food.

Then leaning on the mantelshelf
As though a mountain now myself
I smoked with mist and dripped with rain
That slowly made me dry again.

Morning in the Combe

The low sun halves the combe,
One side in sunlight, one in gloom,
And where they meet together
I walk from winter into summer weather.

There hard mud kept the cast
Of hoof and claw and foot that passed,
While here I stumble over
Moist earth that draws me backward like a lover.

The Archaeologist

Although men may dig up
A broken Bacchus with a vine-wreathed cup
Or helmeted chryselephantine goddess;
Though Aphrodite divine and godless,
Helped by a rope, rise from the sea,
None is immortal but Persephone.

See, by an English lane
Cold Hades lets her rise again.
In celandines that in a blaze
Spread like gold starfish their flat rays
Revisiting our earth and sky
Death's wife reveals her immortality.

She glitters with a light
That sharpens, as is said, the swallow's sight;
I am not like that twittering bird;
Too clear a memory my eyes has blurred;
Not this side heaven I'll see again
As once I saw it, a gold English lane.

Hibernating Snails

Here where the castle faces south
The ivy spreading its flat tree
Hides snails in heaps thick and uncouth,
All fast asleep with open mouth,
Although they breathe no air,
Each china throat sealed up with glair;
Yet some will never wake at all,
For two years old or even three
They crawled alive to their own funeral.

The Flesh-Scraper

If I had sight enough
Might I not find a fingerprint
Left on this flint
By Neolithic man or Kelt?
So knapped to scrape a wild beast's pelt,
The thumb below, fingers above,
See, my hand fits it like a glove.

A Prospect of Death

If it should come to this,
You cannot wake me with a kiss,
Think I but sleep too late
Or once again keep a cold angry state.

So now you have been told; –
I or my breakfast may grow cold,
But you must only say
'Why does he miss the best part of the day?'

Even then you may be wrong;
Through woods torn by a blackbird's song
My thoughts may often roam
While graver business makes me stay at home.

There will be time enough
To go back to the earth I love
Some other day that week,
Perhaps to find what all my life I seek.

So do not dream of danger;
Forgive my lateness or my anger;
You have so much forgiven,
Forgive me this or that, or Hell or Heaven.

The Dunes

These heavy hills of sand,
That marram-grasses bind
Lest they should fly off on the wind,
Hold back the sea from Sea-kings' Land.

Such a waste holds me too
From fields where shadows fly,
Wolds, woods and streams that quote the sky,
All the sweet country that is you.

Christmas Day

Last night in the open shippen
   The Infant Jesus lay,
While cows stood at the hay-crib
   Twitching the sweet hay.

As I trudged through the snow-fields
   That lay in their own light,
A thorn-bush with its shadow
   Stood doubled on the night.

And I stayed on my journey
   To listen to the cheep
Of a small bird in the thorn-bush
   I woke from its puffed sleep.

The bright stars were my angels
   And with the heavenly host
I sang praise to the Father,
   The Son and Holy Ghost.

The Stone Eagles

Purple and gold and wet
   To Toller Fratrum, Wynyard Eagle,
Both roads in the sunset
   Shone with a light so rich and regal;
Which choose without regret?

Chance led me by the one
   Where two lean-headed eagles perched
Rain-pitted to the bone
   And the last dregs of daylight searched
With their blind eyes of stone.

What were they watching for?
   Wild eagles that again would fly
Over a waste land or
   Scything wide circles in the sky
Mechanic birds of war?

Essex Salt-Marsh

Now the tide's task is done,
Marsh runnels turn and chuckling run
Or come to a standstill,
The level ground for them a breathless hill.

And as they run or faint
Through mud that takes the sunset's paint,
The gullies they have worn
Shine as with purple grapes and golden corn.

The Cuillin Hills

Each step a cataract of stones
So that I rise and sink at once,
Slowly up to the ridge I creep;
And as through drifting smoke
Of mist grey-black as a hoodie-crow
The ghostly boulders come and go
And two hoarse ravens croak
That hopped with flapping wings by a dead sheep,
All is so hideous that I know
It would not kill me though I fell
A thousand feet below;
On you, Black Cuillin, I am now in hell.

Overtaken by Mist

Like lightning on the mountain-slope
The stalker's path zigzagged,
And climbing it with steps that lagged
I often raised my eyes in hope
To where Scour Ouran's head was bare;
But mist that gathered from nowhere
With a bright darkness filled the air,
Until, both earth and heaven gone,
Never was man or angel so alone.

Beaulieu River

Largest of Forest snakes, by heath and scrog
It stretches in its blue sky-borrowed coat,
For while its tail trails in a cotton bog
It grips with foaming mouth the Solent's throat.

Walking on the Cliff

But for a sleepy gull that yawned
    And spread its wings and dropping disappeared
This evening would have dawned
    To the eternity my flesh has feared.

For too intent on a blackcap
    Perched like a miser on the yellow furze
High over Birling Gap,
    That sang 'Gold is a blessing not a curse',

How near I was to stepping over
    The brink where the gull dropped to soar beneath,
While now safe as a lover
    I walk the cliff-edge arm in arm with Death.

The Green Man
(1947)

Hard Frost

Frost called to water 'Halt!'
And crusted the moist snow with sparkling salt;
Brooks, their own bridges, stop,
And icicles in long stalactites drop,
And tench in water-holes
Lurk under gluey glass like fish in bowls.

In the hard-rutted lane
At every footstep breaks a brittle pane,
And tinkling trees ice-bound,
Changed into weeping willows, sweep the ground;
Dead boughs take root in ponds
And ferns on windows shoot their ghostly fronds.

But vainly the fierce frost
Interns poor fish, ranks trees in an armed host,
Hangs daggers from house-eaves
And on the windows ferny ambush weaves;
In the long war grown warmer
The sun will strike him dead and strip his armour.

Sudden Thaw

When day dawned with unusual light,
Hedges in snow stood half their height
And in the white-paved village street
Children were walking without feet.

But now by their own breath kept warm
Muck-heaps are naked at the farm
And even through the shrinking snow
Dead bents and thistles start to grow.

In Avebury Circle

I see the white clouds blow
From cottages thick-thatched with snow
More clearly than I read
This great stone monster without feet, wings, head:

A huge night-blackening shadow
Set up by kings in this holy meadow,
Where of his fellows most
With those antique Cimmerians are lost.

I wonder if King Sil
Will rise and ride from Silbury Hill,
Where buried with his horse
He sits, a strange invulnerable corse,

And grey wethers that keep
On Clatford Down their lichened sleep
Drive to this ancient fold
And bring again an age of stone and gold.

A Sussex Ghyll

Primroses thick on its steep floor,
This ghyll deserves a better door
Than an old doubled sack
Flung over the barbed fence's narrow back.

The stream has its own way to come;
And though leaves try to keep it dumb
And even choke it dead,
Like a sick man it lies and sings in bed.

The trees are old: some ivy climbs;
Others like lepers drop their limbs;
But this stream delved the ghyll
Till each bank 'Good-bye' said – a distant hill.

The Dead Sheep

There was a blacksmith in my breast,
That worked the bellows of my chest
    And hammer of my heart,
As up the heavy scree I pressed,
    Making the loose stones scream, crag-echoes start.

Rocks, rising, showed that they were sheep,
But one remained as though asleep,
    And how it was I saw,
When loath to leave the huddled heap
    A hoodie crow rose up with angry craw.

Though stiller than a stone it lay,
The face with skin half-flayed away
    And precious jewels gone,
The eye-pits darted a dark ray
    That searched me to my shadowy skeleton.

The Nightingale and Owl

How often had I tried to see
A nightingale, and only seen the tree;
Tonight I went with new belief
That I should see one, looking leaf by leaf.

And I was glad too that I went,
For as I listened, drinking the may's scent,
Another came, drawn by the tale
Of that Greek girl changed to a nightingale.

O Philomela, but for me
Who frightened that dark shadow from the tree,
A further change you had gone through,
Your 'Tereu-tereu' now 'Too-whit too-whoo'!

Field-Glasses

Though buds still speak in hints
And frozen ground has set the flints
As fast as precious stones
And birds perch on the boughs, silent as cones,

Suddenly waked from sloth
Young trees put on a ten years' growth
And stones double their size,
Drawn nearer through field-glasses' greater eyes.

Why I borrow their sight
Is not to give small birds a fright
Creeping up close by inches;
I make the trees come, bringing tits and finches.

I lift a field itself
As lightly as I might a shelf,
And the rooks do not rage
Caught for a moment in my crystal cage.

And while I stand and look,
Their private lives an open book,
I feel so privileged
My shoulders prick, as though they were half-fledged.

Prospect of a Mountain

Though cuckoos call across the kyle
And larks are dancing everywhere
To their thin bagpipe's air,
My thoughts are of the autumn day
I climbed that Quinaig, monstrous pile,
And striding up its slaggy brow
Stood outside time and space;
It looks so empty of me now,
More years than miles away,
The mountain-cairn might mark my burial-place.

In Moonlight

Rain pattered in the poplar trees,
    And yet there was no rain;
It was clear moon; the trees' unease
    Made me hear water plain.

It seemed that lover walked by lover
    So sharp my shadow showed;
We never needed to step over
    The tree-trunks on the road.

The moon too on the other side
    From tree to tree flew on,
As though she had forsook the tide
    For her Endymion.

The truest lovers I could have –
    So to myself I said –
The shadow marking out my grave
    And moon lending a spade.

Spring Flowers

Now we enjoy the rain,
When at each neighbour's door we hear
'How big primroses are this year' –
Tale we may live to hear again –

And dandelions flood
The orchards as though apple-trees
Dropped in the grass ripe oranges,
Boughs still in pink impatient bud,

When too we cannot choose,
But one foot and the other set
In celandine and violet,
Walking in gold and purple shoes,

Rain that through winter weeks
Splashed on our face and window pane,
And rising in these flowers again
Brightens their eyes and fats their cheeks.

The Blind Children

Where caterpillars ate their fill
On hazels' mealy leaves until
The boughs were stript half-bare
And leaves hung riddled with clear holes of air,

I met with children who upturned
Faces to where the blue sky burned,
Some blinking in the glare,
Some looking up with a white open stare.

I did not need to question which
Should leave the road and take the ditch;
I felt it was small kindness
To children walking arm in arm in blindness.

From their blind eyes I borrowed sight
To see the leaves against the light
Rich and not ruinous,
Set with bright diamonds on the fire-fringed boughs.

May Frost

It was the night May robbed September
Killing with frost the apple-bloom,
The sunset sunk to its last ember,
I climbed the dew-webbed combe;
There floating from the earth's round rim
I saw the red sun rise.
At first I only thought 'How soon',
And then 'Surely I must be dying;
These are death's cobwebs on my eyes
That make the dawn so dim';
And yet my sight was lying:
The frost had set on fire the full-faced moon.

The Blind Man

Speak of the birds, he lifts a listening finger
And 'chiff-chaff' 'willow-warbler' names each singer,
'Hedge-sparrow' 'robin' 'wren'; he knows their cries,
Though all are nightingales to his blind eyes.

A Mountain Graveyard

Sheep-fold, I thought – till by the dyke
    I saw it lying deep in dock
And knew he never whistled tyke,
    The herd who folded that quiet flock.

The Beech-Wood

When the long, varnished buds of beech
Point out beyond their reach,
And tanned by summer suns
Leaves of black bryony turn bronze,
And gossamer floats bright and wet
From trees that are their own sunset,
Spring, summer, autumn I come here,
And what is there to fear?
And yet I never lose the feeling
That someone close behind is stealing
Or else in front has disappeared;
Though nothing I have seen or heard,
The fear of what I might have met
Makes me still walk beneath these boughs
With cautious steps as in a haunted house.

On the Hillside

What causes the surprise
That greets me here under the piecemeal skies
Of this thick-wooded scar?
Is it the look that the familiar
Keeps as of something strange
When so much else is constant but to change?
No, it's the thought that this white sun that cleaves
A silvery passage through the leaves
Is the same sun that cleft them
A week ago, as though I never left them
And never went in the sad interval
To my friend's funeral,
Though crossing the churchyard today I shivered
To see how fast on a fresh grave the flowers had withered.

The Rockland Broad

Water too clear to show,
Unless a frown ruffle its brow,
I scarcely feel afloat –
I am suspended in a flying-boat!

Sure, with the land so low
This broad will burst and overflow,
Rush on and never stop,
Till the whole world becomes one water-drop.

Though willow-carrs and reeds
And alders, too, change to seaweeds,
Let Heaven again take note,
Save this new Noah in his flying-boat.

Lady's Slipper Orchid

Though I know well enough
To hunt the Lady's Slipper now
Is playing blindman's-buff,
For it was June She put it on
And grey with mist the spiders' lace
Swings in the autumn wind,
Yet through this hill-wood, high and low,
I peer in every place;
Seeking for what I cannot find
I do as I have often done
And shall do while I stay beneath the sun.

The Salmon-Leap

Leaves, and not birds, now flit,
Brighter than yellow wagtail and coal-tit,
Or on the water lie
Making a sunset of the fishes' sky.

Autumn for salmon-trout
Is spring, and Io Hymen boulders shout,
Spate drawing them to spawn
Where on high hills the river keeps its dawn.

From rock-lipt lynn to lynn,
Shaking the ferns and grasses with their din,
The cascades overflow
And pour in pools to rise as boiling snow;

Tossing their bodies bare
The salmon-trout are seen tasting our air,
For stronger is the flood
That rages in their few small drops of blood.

Dundonnel Mountains

Through mist that sets the hills on fire
And rising, never rises higher
Looms a stone figure, gross and squat,
An idol carved out by the weather,
Face, limbs and body lumped together;
And while for none but mountain fox
Eagle or buzzard or wild cat
Its worship may be orthodox,
Death fawning on me from these rocks,
A false step would suffice
To make me both its priest and sacrifice.

In Burnham Beeches

Walking among these smooth beech-boles
   With cracks and galls
And beetle-holes
   And ivy trickling in green waterfalls,

I noted carvings on their barks,
   Faint and diffuse
As china-marks
   On Worcester or Old Bow: I wondered whose.

I feared that time had played its part
   With those whose token
Was a twin heart,
   So many hearts the swelling bark had broken.

The Haystack

Too dense to have a door,
Window or fireplace or a floor,
They saw this cottage up,
Huge bricks of grass, clover and buttercup
Carting to byre and stable,
Where cow and horse will eat wall, roof and gable.

110

The Revenant

O foolish birds, be dumb,
   And you, jay, stop your mocking laughter;
A revenant I come
   Today as I might come fifty years after.

Why, birds, I am no stranger,
   For as I cross the copse and back,
I feel a double-ganger,
   Who meets himself at each turn of the track.

A better welcome give
   To one who may have bent and blessed
Your fathers four or five
   Laid in the smooth round hollow of a nest.

Come less than fifty years,
   Owls may have cause to mock at one
Who stalks this wood and wears
   A frosty coat that will not stand the sun.

In Breckland

Why is it when I cross the warren,
That last year's thistles make more barren,
Rabbits standing upright like men
Dive in their holes again,
And turtle that to turtle purrs
Rises and swerves from the blue belt of firs,
And even the mole that works beneath
Like a small earthquake holds its breath?
Hated by all for others' sins
I bless this rat that only grins,
Stayed by the stiff indifference of death.

A Dead Bird

Finding the feathers of a bird
Killed by a sparrow-hawk,
I thought, What need is there to walk?
And bound them on my feet;
And as I flew off through the air,
I saw men stare up from a street
And women clasp their hands in prayer.
'To Hades' was no sooner said
Than a winged Hermes I was there;
And though I peered round for the dead,
Nothing I saw and nothing heard
But a low moaning from a bough,
'Ah, who is wearing my poor feathers now?'

The Shower

The cherry-pickers left their picking
And ladders through the branches sticking
And cherries hung like gouts of blood
Down the long aisles of white-washed wood.

But now the sun is breaking through
Dark clouds that dry to pools of blue
And the smooth Medway lies uncreased
Except for drops the boughs released.

What is it makes the sun so proud
He will not suck a passing cloud
But needs raindrops to quench his thirst?
Well, let him do his picking first.

At Amberley Wild Brooks

Watching the horses stand
And bend their long heads Roman-nosed,
With thick cheek veins exposed,
So close to where the brook's bank shelves
They almost meet themselves
In the smooth water sliding by,
I think it strange creatures so great
Can be shut in by wooden gate
And brook no deeper than my hand,
And not like Pegasus shoot wings and fly.

Cornish Flower-Farm

Here where the cliff rises so high
The sea below fills half the sky
And ships hang in mid-air,
Set on the cliff-face, square by square,
Walls of veronica enclose
White gladioli in their neat rows
And blue and golden irises;
But though the walls grow tall as trees,
Some flowers from their quiet quillets pass
To mix with wayside weeds and grass,
Like nuns that from their strict retreats
Go visiting the poor in their plain streets.

The Shepherd's Hut

The smear of blue peat smoke
That staggered on the wind and broke,
The only sign of life,
Where was the shepherd's wife,
Who left those flapping clothes to dry,
Taking no thought for her family?
For, as they bellied out
And limbs took shape and waved about,
I thought, She little knows
That ghosts are trying on her children's clothes.

On the Common

The chaffy seeds by the wind blown
Are here so strangely sown,
That one might almost say
The spider's-webs the bushes wear
Have been put down to hay,
And though no crop they bear
Ploughed and cross-ploughed on empty air,
So thick these hay-fields swarm,
That every gorse-bush is become a farm.

By the Erme

No trace of absent years
Water or bank or boulder wears;
All is the same as when I went away.

Even my floating face
Seems looking up from the same place,
More steadfast than the stream that cannot stay.

I might have left it there,
Although I notice that my hair
Now stirs a little foam in the smooth bay.

At Formby

From that wide empty shore,
No foot had ever trod before
(Or since the sea drew back the tide),
I climbed the dune's soft slide
To where no higher than my hand
Wind-bitten pines grew in the clogging sand.

But farther from the beach
The trees rose up beyond my reach,
And as I walked, they still grew taller
And I myself smaller and smaller,
Till gazing up at a high wood
I felt that I had found my lost childhood.

View from Mountain

When through the parting mist,
That the sun's warm gold mouth had kissed,
The hills beneath me came to view
With lochans gleaming here and there,
It was not like the earth I knew;
Another world was shining through,
As though that earth had worn so thin
I saw the living spirit within,
Its beauty almost pain to bear
Waking in me the thought,
If heaven by act of death were brought
Nearer than now, might I not die
Slain by my immortality?

A Shot Magpie

Though on your long-tailed flight
You wore half-mourning of staid black and white,
So little did the thought of death
Enter your thievish head,
You never knew what choked your breath
When in a day turned night
You fell with feathers heavier than lead.

The Swedes

Three that are one since time began,
Horse, cart and man,
Lurch down the lane patched with loose stones;
Swedes in the cart heaped smooth and round
Like skulls that from the ground
The man has dug without the bones
Leave me in doubt
Whether the swedes with gold shoots sprout
Or with fresh fancies bursts each old bald sconce.

The Mud

This glistening mud that loves a gate
Was mashed by cows of late,
But now its puddles lie so still
They hold the clouds and trees and hill;

But when the painted cows come out
From milking-shed to grass
And churn the mud up as they pass,
How cloud and tree and hill will dart about!

The Day Ends

The day ends and its heat
Lies in chill dews about our feet;
But though its twelve hours seemed as soon
Gone as the twelve strokes struck at noon,
So much those hours have freed
To blow away for memory's seed,
Will they not still be ours,
Fixed like the church-tower's gilt and holy hours?

Twilight

As daylight drains away
And darkness creeps out of the wood
And flowers become too faint to tell,
My eyesight failing me as well
And chill dew watering my blood,
I might imagine night was my last day.

But why need I rehearse
What I must play with my whole heart?
Spectators may be moved to tears
To see me act these now-feigned fears;
While others summing up the part
May with approval say, His lines were terse.

from

Out of the World and Back
(1958)

Into Hades

1 *The Funeral*

One midnight in the Paris Underground
Walking along the tunnel to a train,
I saw a man leaning against the wall,
Eyes shut, head sunk on chest; selling newspapers
He had fallen asleep, but still stood on his feet.
Just so I must have stood,
When drowsily I heard, as from a distance,
Forasmuch – Almighty God – unto himself
The soul of our dear brother here departed,
We therefore commit his body to the ground;
Earth to earth, ashes to ashes – Half-asleep,
My mind took time to gather in the meaning;
Than I began to wonder, and awoke.

        By an open grave
Lined with the undertaker's verdant grass,
Their backs toward me, priest and people stood.
The verger, who dropped the clods, dusting his hands,
Why, it was Fred! And this was Stonegate Church!
These were my friends, the priest the Rural Dean;
Did they think I lay ill in the vicarage,
Too ill to bury a parishioner?
Could they not see me standing in the road?
But when I saw the Three,
Who after the priest's *'I heard a voice from heaven'*
Drew closer to the grave's brink and gazed down,

I gasped and cried, 'Stop! there is some mistake;
You cannot bury me; I am not dead'.
But no one turned, for no one heard my cry.
Terrified by the silence of my own voice,
I sank down with a shudder by the lych-gate.

2   *The Prison*

        It was like waking
In a strange room; I almost hoped to hear
The opening of a door, a slippered step.
The funeral came slowly back as though
A scene from last night's play. I lay and listened
For night's stealthy noises, swaying curtain,
Sigh of spent cinders in a fire-place; but all
Was silent as myself. No wind outside
Drew its loose fingers through a bush; farm-cock
Still slept like weather-cock.
But I could wait. Soon a window would grow pale;
Already I could see my hand, my body.
I had no fear, thinking of nothing more
Than the strange novelty of being dead.

        Often I had waked
Thankful to be alive after an air-raid;
I was as thankful now to wake and to be dead.
I even grew light-headed; I had made
The long night journey in a sleeping carriage;
I had not changed at Crewe. Where was my watch?
What was the time now in Eternity?
The funeral was a hoax; how false that coffin
They slowly lowered with its puppet. Why,
It was my conjurer's box, with which I showed
The Vanishing Parson; played the trick so well
I had deceived myself. Scared by the audience,
Affected by the flowers, unconscious bouquets,
I had been seized by stage-fright and cried out,
'You cannot bury me; I am not dead'.

Would someone come?
The place must have its routine, a new arrival
Causing no sensation. I should hear voices soon,
Friends at the door. Which should we be in heaven,
Our parents' children or our children's parents?
We might be both. Time could be a clock,
No foolish face, only a pendulum,
Swinging us to and fro, backward and forward,
From age to youth, from youth again to age,
The psychological clock our minds had lived by
In the interchange of memory and hope.

This dusk was ambiguous;
Would it thin to dawn or thicken to darkness? I waited,
Longing to hear a bird's first doubtful chirp
And then another and the whole kindled chorus.
But no birds sang that morning – if it was morning.
Birds had no time to sing, for while my eyes
Were fumbling with informal cloudy shapes,
Light entered with a step, and it was day,
Wide-open, unabashed. I stared in wonder
At what had the appearance of a prison
With thick-ribbed vault and iron-studded door.
Yet it seemed hardly real;
More like a dungeon in an opera,
Fidelio or *Faust*. What made it stranger,
I saw no window for the light to enter.

Frightened, yet half mocking,
I sat and viewed it. Was this one of those fits
That often seized me? Objects of themselves
Melted away to their own images,
An insubstantial world; or it only needed
That I should say, 'I see what I am seeing',
To feel that what I looked on was unreal,
Nothing was changed, but all was visionary,
And I was in a waking dream. But this time
My sight was in reverse and what looked real
Was visionary. Reaching out my hand
To put it to the proof, I touched a stone;

It was as soft as mist; my hand went through it,
Boring a hole. This was mere make-believe,
Stuff of myself; like a silkworm I had spun
My own cocoon. I understood this prison;
A symbol of the womb, it was the presage
Of my new birth. No midwife would be needed
For this confinement; precocious embryo,
I should prick the pregnant bubble. These stones would vanish,
The prisoner escaping with the prison.

          From this side death
Ghost tales seemed credible; could I not go back
To the vicarage? show myself to the Three,
Who thought they left me in the lowered box?
Would they be psychic? A determined ghost,
I should be palpable, besiege the house,
Lay ambushes in the garden, look through a window –
But at the thought I stiffened!
A picture came to my mind – was it from something
I had seen or read? or was it not imagined? –
Of a dead man, live ghost, who came and stood
Outside a lighted window of his house,
Face crushed against the glass, white as a mushroom,
Eyes burning like a moth's, and gazed within
On wife and children, who were so unconscious
A daughter rose and looked out on the darkness
And, seeing nothing, drew the blind. I was frightened
By that picture so intolerant of hope;
It even woke new fear.

3   *The Body*

        I had seen a tree-trunk,
That hurt the ground with its dead weight, sprout leaves
Not knowing it was dead; I had caught fish,
Flounders that flapped, eels tying and untying
Slippery knots, slow to drown in our air;
Was I too living out my life's last remnant,
Not living, only lasting? Was Death a monster,

A cat that toyed with a mouse, caught but not killed?
The thought seized my brain, a fear so tumultuous
That, afraid of itself, it died in fascination,
A crouching, a yielding to the softened paw,
The sense I was safe – not to escape.

        Or was I not yet myself,
Not recovered from my illness, cured by death,
Still convalescent? How had I died?
Had death come as a storm, tornado, razing
A tract of memory? There was a gap,
Days, weeks and months torn from the almanac.
I remembered my father's death;
How I had watched the hard, humiliating struggle,
That made me half ashamed that I, his son,
Spied on his weakness. I remembered her,
Who held her son's last letter in her hand
Like a passport to heaven. I remembered too
Thinking that some time I should go their way;
But had I then believed it?

        Why, even now
The sight and touch of my accustomed body
Compromised the truth. Here it was out of place,
An obvious mistake. Raising my hand
I recognized a white scar on my wrist;
I felt my heart; shut in its cage of bones,
That songless lark kept time. But the funeral!
The coffin with its cargo! I was confused;
Were there two bodies, two scars, two bird-cages?
Paudricia in *Palmerin of England*
In place of her lover, still alive in prison,
Buried his effigy. Trust the undertaker
Not to bury a guy.

        As I looked at my body,
It stared back with a strange impertinence,
Familiar, hostile, superfluous proof I was dead.
It, too, was make-believe, stuff of myself,
Old use and wont expected, therefore seen.

I was my own Pygmalion!
A fungoid outgrowth, it was not like that other
I left in the churchyard, that stiff, straight soldier
Who kept good guard in his fallen sentry-box.

I must not sleep again;
Nothing to hold it, my body would be gone,
And, body gone, should I not also go?
The thought alarmed me; it was high time to answer
The long-unanswered knocking at my mind's
Back-door. I had heard it since I first awoke,
Steady as a clocklike dripping in a crypt.
Now I bustled about and with shamefaced 'Welcome, stranger,
You should have come up by the garden path',
I greeted my terrific visitor,
The thought of God.

4   *The Prisoner*

The thought was surgical,
But could I not disarm it of the knife?
Had I no grievance I had been kept waiting
So long in an ante-room? *O bona Patria,*
Num tua gaudia teque videbo?
How often had I sung. Not patriotic
Like Bernard de Morlaix, I yet had tasted
The honey of the land in his sweet *Rhythm.*
Where was that land? where was the mystic city?
What had I seen? A ghost with a white scar,
An opera prison.

But nothing happened,
Time lazy, stale, dammed up by a long moment.
Was I here forever, or till the Judgment Day?
Which was this cell, convict's or anchorite's?
The prison irked me; though it looked determined,
It was stage property. What I had conjured up
Could I not conjure down? Calling to myself,
'These are the prophet's stones of emptiness',

I tried to wave it away. It answered back,
Stones shooting out on elongated necks
Fantastic gargoyles. It was like a church
Turned outside in. Waving their serpent heads,
They reached towards me, tugging at the walls;
I was seized by my oldest fear, to be buried alive,
And gave a nightmare cry.

 I outstared them in the end;
Grinning acknowledgment, they relapsed to stone.
I was their Gorgon's head!
Yet I was afraid; it was dangerous to be dead.

5 *The Lover*

 Why had I waked?
There was no future in this future life,
Nothing to do, no prayer, no repentance.
Dante set out to walk from hell to heaven
For his soul's health, but mine had caught a cold.
And Dante came back! Why was I singled out?
What was peculiar? What the truth, the value?
Was it in that young lover,
Who pitched his tent in heaven and read Plato?

 I had the strange feeling
Someone that moment, in looking through my relics,
Had found a ring, a ring of twisted silver
Carved with a letter, and had paused to wonder
Whose name it stood for, what the cheap treasure meant.
How little did he guess
She had been nothing I could see or touch
And had no other name than that I gave her
Unless among the angels. Unlike Psyche
Lighting her penny dip, I asked no sight
Of the flying Eros. Hermits and virgins,
Who in the love and proof of chastity
Slept side by side in the Egyptian desert,
Had not so pure a passion. Joseph and Mary

Might have been the witnesses, when at our wedding
I placed the ring, for our marriage was by proxy,
On the third finger – of my own left hand.

Her speech a responsive silence,
(Though in undertones of streams I caught her voice),
She was the charm of woods, my Adam's rib,
My Muse, my shadow on the sunny side.
She mocked me on mountains; where hands and knees clasped rocks.
She glided as a ghost; yet in a mist's
Rich loneliness she was singularly present.
I found her most in Paris;
In the twilight, in the evening, when, behold,
A woman at the corner, she cooled my blood
More than the corpses set up in the Morgue
Like fashion dummies in a milliner's window.
I starved my body that the loosened spirit
Might break out to the prospect, the fulfilment;
Indulged in the thought of death, feeding on Plato;
For though he argued of the life to come
With only half his head, he was himself
The better argument.

With no gross brain
Steadying it, my mind clutched at a hope;
Though I had broken my noviciate's vows,
Fallen from that envied self, now my despair,
Might she not trespass on a timid star
And, euphrasy on her eyes, see how her lover
Struggled in this strait-jacket? That Platonic love
Was withered seaweed, crawled over by bleached dead crabs,
Busy with sand-hoppers; yet it had floated once,
Waved with the water, lustrous, stranger than earthplant.
Believe what you see not and you shall see
What you will not believe: If in the words
There was heavenly logic, might she not come?
I outbid hope; she would come laughing, mocking
My artificial body, 'not one true limb,
Poor Dresden china shepherd'. But what came instead
Was sleep, an irresistible sleep –

Morning was late that day,
Delayed by thick fog. Trees, their tops out of sight,
Scattered irregular rain: dew-hoary cobwebs
Drooped with false geometry. Over the hedge
The mist drew round the coats of coughing sheep
A halo of silver light: they might have been
Hyperion's. How I came in the garden
Was denser fog. A moorhen on the pond,
Jetting its head with red phylactery,
Pushed forward in widening angles. Seeing a man,
It would have croaked and run with dripping legs
To shelter in the reeds: but it swam closer.
I was a ghost; I could go up to birds
And pick them like a barn-owl from a bough.
That it was my own garden I was haunting
Filled it with stinging nettles. The old boat,
Upturned with gaping wounds, was not so dead;
It came to life in summer, growing warm
And raising tarry blisters.

The sun itself was a ghost,
A pallid ball that came and went in the haze
It helped to thin. I saw the vicarage
Across the pond; but where was my ambition
To haunt it? Achilles' horses could shed tears,
But mine were raindrops on a winter bough,
That freeze and forget to fall. For something told me
I was warned away, a trespasser in my own garden.
I had come home to learn
With how true an instinct I had dedicated
The ring of twisted silver in the end.

The bell rang for the Celebration.
It had an absent sound, but I would be present;
All mornings for a ghost were All Saints' Night.
Why, when they brought St Germain's body to church,
Choir tapers lit themselves. And I wore my cassock!
Had they buried me like a Carthusian monk

In his usual habit? And the feast was ghostly;
I should feel at home, see with St Chrysostom
The Word born on the altar; I should kneel
And worship like the Magi at the manger.

        The bell stopped ringing,
As I took the road. The boy with Sunday papers
Came cycling down; I would have said 'Good morning',
But he rode past, eyes fixed ahead. I turned
And saw him jump off at the garden gate
And, feeling for a paper, disappear.
He had looked through my body! The hedge was thorny;
I clawed it, eager for the sight of blood
As the thronging ghosts Odysseus drove with his sword
From the red pool. But I was an empty ghost
And no blood came. I had seen Death at last:
He had ridden past me, not on his pale horse,
But on a cycle with the *Sunday Times*.

        It mattered little
The service was begun. The Ten Commandments
I could take as read – what were they to me now? –
Omit the Offertory – silver and gold,
Could I not say, with Peter, I had none?
Reaching the lych-gate, where at first I fainted,
I almost fainted again. As I stole a glance
At the white chrysanthemums that buried my grave,
The sun made rainbows on my wet eye-lashes.
Lift up your hearts, I heard; but my heart sank;
My ghostly hands had not strength enough to turn
The door's iron handle. I darted to a window;
But the priest was not in view. I outdid Zacchaeus;
Overflying the roof, I perched on an Irish yew,
That grew on the farther side against the chancel.
The priest was kneeling: like God or an eavesdropper
I knew the words he spoke. At the Consecration,
When he stood with hovering hands over the Birth,
I watched him like a young communicant,
Who through his fingers spies on the priest's action.
But when he raised the Host,

The Bread that feeds us as we feed the Bread,
He straightened upwards in a fearful elongation,
Tall as a seraph. I gazed at him aghast
As at the sight of something that could not happen.
My trembling shook the tree. Then all grew dim,
Cloudy, tumultuous, a swirling smoke.
'Fire! your church is on fire!' I almost cried
To the sleeping villagers, but I remembered
The prophet's words, *The house was filled with smoke.*
As the candle flames, indignant eyes, burned through it,
I slid down from the tree; not church, but churchyard,
Fitted a ghost. I was excommunicated.

7   Mattins

                    The fog had left the sun
A heavy dew to lift; Thomson, the farmer,
Trailed a dark track in the cow-pasture. But I,
A ghost, a little fog myself, trailed none
Through the churchyard grass. Shunning chrysanthemums,
I sat on a flat stone, alive with lichen.
It might have been a moonbeam the sun cast,
For I felt no warmth.

                    Locked out by St Peter's key!
And from the church that he and I had shared
As patron saint and priest! I was the more
Aggrieved, for churches were my love and study,
Not theology. I sat and wrapt myself
In their warm memory, from Norman naves,
Huge monsters standing on elephantine legs,
Tame at the altar, to the little churches
With scarcely room for God. Stone foliage
Showed me the spring in winter at West Walton,
Angels smiled down as they spread their wooden wings
To fly off with Knapton's roof. I thought of Gloucester,
Where under the swirling fan-vault of the cloister
I walked like a river-god; of Beverley's
Dense forest of choir stalls, where I unearthed

Strange creatures, salamanders, unicorns,
Peacocks and men whose faces were their bellies.
Lincoln's rose-window so hurt me with its beauty,
It was like broken glass; sun shining through,
Apollo was a Christian.

Was the church a well,
That filled from within? I had seen no people enter,
Yet voices sang to the organ. They sang *Venite*,
But I did not come; I sat, too, through the Psalms
Like an invalid. Gazing about the churchyard,
I saw it was autumn; berries on the hedge
Hung in bright bracelets; bryony, nightshade, how vain
To remember the names. A silence grew more than silence,
A vacuum, that drew me to a window.
One of my friends stood at the lectern eagle;
Jove's messenger, the brazen bird looked bored,
It had so often listened to the Lessons.
As I peered at the priest, the stranger in my stall,
The congregation rose, filling the church
For the *Te Deum*. So they must have risen,
When I was shouldered out, smothered with flowers
To make my death the surer. The thought was bitter;
It turned the *Te Deum* to the *Nunc Dimittis*.
Two women stood at the other side of the window;
I could have touched the nearer but for the glass
And a lost world between. Turning her head,
She stared at me in wonder. Would she start the story
She had seen her late vicar's ghost? Though I told myself
I was only another window she looked through,
I stole from the church's shadow.

The white chrysanthemums
Seduced my feet. I stood over my grave
At the priest's end. It was my mother Eve,
Apple still in her mouth, who tempted me
To take the plunge into that foaming gulf.
I saw a wonder: the coffin-lid mere glass,
I gazed down at the gaunt philosopher.
I hardly knew myself; here was a change

From Epicurean to the Stoic school.
But the coffin was a trap; springing to life
He rose, a towering wave of lust, and gripped me;
I choked in his close embrace, cold awful kiss.

8 *World's End*

        It was touch and go,
That I escaped the shaking of the sheet,
The breathless suction, being buried in my grave.
Corpses so amorous, earth was not safe
For wandering ghosts. The prison would be safer,
No fear of being murdered by a dead man.
But was I back in prison?
I gazed on nothing; even the floor had fled;
The prison, not the prisoner, had escaped!
All was so absent, I had the baffled sense
That in looking I did not look. It was like a sea
Without the water. Hung on a spacious point,
I feared to stretch a hand; I might overbalance,
Fall without end; it was dangerous as a dream.
I viewed myself with distaste. Emphatic Ego,
A speck of horrible conspicuousness,
I felt exposed. Shaming the one-eyed Cyclops,
I borrowed the whole universe for eye,
A gazing-stock to myself.

        Flowing ectoplasm,
This body would not last, not even as long
As that other body lying in its sunk boat,
Shipwrecked on land. This was a replica,
That the original. I felt for its defeat
A self-pity: face that had hoisted the white flag
To the invaders; veins, once fruitful rivers,
Stagnant canals; the heart, that had kept good time,
Stopped; inner works, that had gone of their own accord,
While I, the engineer, had walked on deck,
Run down; the precious idol that all my life
I had fed with hecatombs of sheep and oxen,

Given rich libations, fallen. Though the Creed
Spoke of an exhumation and Coroner's inquest,
It lay in a world that itself had fallen to nothing.
I was further from that world than the nebulae,
Not space enough between us to drop a pin.
Trout in time's stream, nosing its solid wind,
Helped by a heavenly hook, I had leapt out
And landed on the bank.

9   *The Rainbow*

           Was I near the Magnetic Mountain,
Climbed by those saints who, wounded by love's arrow,
Had sought for healing at their Hunter's wounds?
Rapt from themselves to a murmuring solitude,
A silent music, they were abroad in bliss,
A merry heat, and tasting marvellous honey,
They loved and burned and shone and in a tempest
Were overthrown. By comprehending not,
They comprehended and in a fathomless staring
Became the light they saw. Through an abyss
That in the Godhead's mountain-range disported,
Beyond activity, wayless and idle,
They passed to a wild estrangement, the Dark Silence
Where all lovers lose themselves.

           Saints were the world's adventure.
I had explored their poor cells of self-knowledge,
Tasted their fasts; my faith leaned hard on theirs,
As substance of things hoped for, evidence
Of things not seen. Now, answering my faith,
The sudden rainbow!

           At first it puzzled my eyes;
Red, orange, green, blue, violet, the names
Did not apply; I could not read the colours
I knew for colours only by their contrast.
It was a rainbow in a foreign language,
If rainbow it was, that overflowed with flowers,

Amorous, dangling in a gay rebellion
From their strict arch. I gazed in frightened joy;
What was to follow, the Book of Revelation
Having opened at this marker? I lay still,
Awed, crouching, tightly clutched by its wide arms,
Eyes drawn up to the supernatural magnet.
Time was not long or short enough to measure
My gazing. Then the strange fires melted.

        My makeshift body, too,
Melted away. My substance was a thought,
That fell back on itself like a wave rising
White on a stream's current. Buoyant, open,
I expatiated in freedom. But not for long;
Too near to nothing, exposed, I craved for objects,
The body's mutual touch, the rough and hard,
A rock's resistance, the boundary of a thorn,
A limit to my false infinitude.

        My thought dropped to the churchyard.
It gaped with an easy earthquake, the coffin-lid
Flying open of itself and the dead man –
Did I catch his action? – pulling back the sheet.
He had drawn his skin-coat tight against the cold
And, pale ascetic, crossed his hands in prayer.
'Brother,' I said, 'I need your blind statue eyes
To see the rainbow's overflowing flowers;
Your deaf ears, so intent, to hear what gospels
Hum round its whispering gallery; a thin hand
To shade me shyly from the Deity.'

        Like the soul of Hermotimus,
Returned from the air to find his body burnt,
I was at a loss. I could have hailed a stone,
Made it an idol; squeezed into a rabbit's burrow
To crush myself to shape. All was so empty,
I was not even defined by what I was not;
I might have flown for ever and not found
A desert. If others like myself were here,
Each had arrived with his own universe.

Whatever it might be after the Judgment,
Our universes now could no more mingle
Than the imaginations of a man and woman
Lying in the same bed.

        Where was my ground,
Support? Trembling, naked, I was an O,
A nothing and a cry of astonishment.
Where there is nothing there is God: the word
Came to my mind; it might have been a flower
Dropt from the rainbow. My sole support was God.
The thought was electric; at the toleration,
God as my unseen, contemplated ground,
My mind began to sparkle.

10   The New Body

        It was a phantom,
Not the true Helen, who was rapt to Egypt,
Paris took to Troy. Phantasmal, too, the body
I lived in, loved on earth; for now the body
I saw, knew as my own, though not yet adopted,
Was real in excess.

        Fantastic coffin,
The boat that bore it slowly sailed in sight,
Lit by St Elmo's fire; it might have come
From anchoring off the rainbow. Solomon's cargo,
The gold and silver, ivory, apes and peacocks,
Was not so precious as that solemn barge's.
Its cargo was its captain, but not dead;
In sleep surmounting sleep he lay in state
Distant, superior, unrecognising,
My new authentic body!
Holy, immortal, my eyes saw it so clearly
They stung me like jelly-fish, as I remembered
How I had profaned its earthly prototype,
Though only a phantom.

I saw it put to shame
The miracle of loaves and fishes. It stirred,
Sprouted with life, rose spreading, multiplying,
Changed to a Jesse-tree. The sleeping Adam
Had more ribs than a wreck: warm, fertile, breathing,
They stretched as boughs, laden with all the bodies
I had worn on earth, child, lover and man.

Gazing at the child,
In whom I saw myself, *O Hesperus,*
That bringest all things back the bright dawn scattered,
I sang with Sappho. Narcissus-like I eyed
The lover who aspired to climb love's ladder;
Petrarch had climbed it, led by Laura's eyes,
But he, who aimed at an eloping angel,
Climbed two or three steps, when beneath his weight
The ladder gave way. The man was multiple,
The one in many, the same, yet different.
I hailed the token! At the Resurrection
It was a changing Proteus who would rise,
Choosing, repeating variable ages,
His life a newel-stair, ascending, descending.

11   *The New Earth*

Caught up to heaven,
Or charmed away by an Orphean lyre,
The tree vanished; it did not even leave
The progenitor. Yet I was not alone;
I knew by the different silence there was an Other,
Invisible, hiding behind himself.
I waited, listened. There was no need to listen:
Silence interpreting itself, the words
Were reflected on my mind like flowers on water,
'Come, see the Bride'. They were as plain as speech,
But whose they were, I had no time to wonder;
As tiny as a thought at first, but growing
To hazel-nut, to apple, to balloon,
A world swam up, losing its shape in size.

If worlds could speak like maps, it would have said,
'The New Earth'.

Her beauty sparkled;
Though I knew her for the old earth, now renewed,
Reborn, she was so transfigured, so unearthly,
I felt I tarnished her even with looking.
All things were conscious, trees talking together,
Streams their own Sirens; mountains might have moved
Slow shoulders. Miraculously as in a dream
She drew close to my side. Distance so near,
Thin as a window-pane, I could have leapt
And landed on her lap, in a laughing ditch
Or cow-gate smiling with subliminal mud.
But I was stuck in space. Not for one lover,
A paralytic too, had this Venus risen.

If the Jesse-tree,
Laden with bodies, a Christmas-tree at Easter,
Had shamed the miracle of loaves and fishes,
What I now saw excelled. It came in glimpses,
As the Earth, a changing Proteus too, repeated
Her variable ages. It flung out
Wild liberty to move both ways in time,
Backward, forward. The moment in reverse,
Past following future, as future followed past,
Clio, playing Penelope's part, would unweave
Her historic web. What sights would be disclosed,
Time ebbing: cities would unbuild themselves,
Temples fly back to their quarries; fossils unfreezing
Would show toothed birds and five-toed horses; coal,
Mining itself, would rise as ferny forests,
Air feel again the weight of flying lizards.
One glimpse I had: it was a dead volcano,
That remembering its old anger, furiously
Stoked its cold fires; perhaps I saw it clearly,
I was so blinded by the frightening flames.

Time's two-way traffic
Would let the apelike man, a sinless satyr,

Loping into the future, view the Parthenon,
While Aristotle, hieing back to the past,
Watched fish that, coming to land, grew legs and lungs.
And myself? I should wander to and fro in time,
Historian of all – its present ages.
I should taste Eternity. Why had I said,
There was no future in this future life?
The New Earth opened out so bright a prospect,
I forgot about its sky!
I looked too late, that strange earth floating away;
But womanlike she tossed me a last word,
'Sun, moon and stars lay in that tomb with Christ'.

12   *The New Heaven*

                Vanished to permanence,
She left a hollow in the emptiness,
That waited to be filled. Should I now hear,
'Come, see the Bridegroom'?
My Monitor – for so I named the Other –
Alarmed me by his stillness. Was he waiting
Prelude, star-signal? The silence grew peculiar,
Then self-assertive, till, swelling immense,
It rocked me as it rose to bursting-point,
To the explosion! I was lifted up,
Dead and alive at once, stunned by a rock,
Assaulted by the sight –

                Plato died in his dream,
But I woke muttering 'The Terrible Crystal'.
What did my lips remember? For my mind
Held nothing real; it was an empty net
Drawn up at night from a phosphorescent sea.
I even felt the distant rainbow frowned
On the effort to remember. I clutched at symbols:
The sky a mirror, feet moving to and fro,
An albatross, a fountain rising in prayer,
One who bent over me, tall as a pillar,
Reflected faces, swaying like flowers, astonished.

Had I scared the angels by my conspicuousness?
Shattered the Crystal?

        I knew with a blind man's feeling
My Monitor was there: I could have kissed
His faithful, invisible feet. He even read
My dumb question, 'Why the earthquake, heavenquake,
The evocation of those foolish symbols?'
The answer came as though written on my mind,
'You flew too high: come, see the saints in flight'.
He proved a Mercury. First his soft rod
Charmed my sick memory asleep; and then!
Argus had fewer eyes shut by that rod
Than I had opened, though in a steadfast sleep.

13   *The Three Hierarchies*

        He rose in flamelike flight,
Singing to music dumb as a music-score
A song inaudible as a bursting rosebud's,
I following in straight ascent. We halted
Where a waterfall, cascade after cascade,
Made an endless thunder. Pools swirled with wondering bubbles
And overflowed in wide columns of water,
That in crashing down stood still. Salmon darkened
Its white tumbling extravagance, leaping out
To fall back, curved like bows, or straight as arrows
Shot through the current. I heard, close as a kiss,
'Look back; see her who sends to heaven these saints,
Missiles, love-letters'. Earth in an empty nadir
Shone like a star reflected in a pool.

        The waterfall stopped,
Salmon hooked in mid-air, the spray a frozen silence;
All was a picture waiting to come alive.
My Monitor called from above, 'Look higher'.
To look was to ascend; I was on a peak,
Exhausted pinnacle. The air was filled
With flying gannets that – Was space upturned?

Why, when they plunged, they rose and fell into the sky,
Not down into a sea. It brought to my mind
How waterdrops fall *up* to a lake's surface
Reflecting drips from an oar. Sharing my thought,
He said, 'Some birds come back; they are not lucky
Like the false water-drops that falling up
Meet their true selves to perish in a kiss.'

       'The Holy Trinity
Is celebrated in three hierarchies;
Come, see the third'. As though at my Monitor's word,
I flew up like a bubble from a stream,
Exploding, lost in air. Yet I gathered myself,
Grew sufficient, and to his mocking 'Look beyond',
I looked. My strained sight took so long to travel,
It might have been climbing an invisible mountain.
But I saw them, even to their gold and purple feathers,
The phoenixes. They struck at the Godhead,
One moment birds and the next moment ashes.
Though they flocked in thousands to their immortal deaths,
Each was God's only phoenix. My Monitor said,
'Yet an archangel's wing, darkening the sky,
Would frighten those small larks'.

       The height relaxing,
I fell away so fast the waterfall
Passed in a flash; I could have overtaken
A stone or shooting star. But I was halted;
The New Earth swam in sight. Rapidly rising,
She burned with an intolerable beauty
That would have scorched my feet, yet seemed each moment
A new creation. She carried her own morning,
A sunny light, to which her heart kept humming.
'Bridegroom waits Bride; the saints will hail the Union,
Inherit both, descending or ascending,
As they see God in creatures or creatures in God',
My Monitor said, and put my dream to sleep.

If he was not myself,
The primal self who never had left heaven,
My Monitor was gone. A ghostly light
Hovered over an open door; it led to a stair,
That invited my downward steps. Though I had played
Ghost in the misty garden, through the window
Watched like a thief the Celebration, stared hard
At the amorous body in his wooden bed,
All had been timeless. The funeral was not finished;
Priest and people would stand by the open grave,
Till I descended the stair.

The light advanced as a torch,
Paving a pale way through my mind's recesses.
It illuminated notions, a knowledge lost
As I stumbled down the faulty, circular stair.
It paused at a window, where sparkling frost-ferns waved,
Commemorating summer. Touched by the torch,
A sudden repentance, they melted in tears. Outside
Floated a misty world I knew by instinct
Was the old earth. It was still in its ancient youth,
Volcanoes bending over it in level smoke,
Foundations settling. In a waste of waters
I discerned the Symbol, shadowy as a shark,
Foreseen, foreseeing, patient without pain,
Jealous and wrathful without perturbation.
The monster would rise, spreading ambitious arms,
Embracing the world, yet empty, Adam's tree,
Leafless, forlorn, clothed with a naked Man,
The Prodigal Son, who came to save the world.

Miscellaneous Short Poems

Landscape

Oppressive with its vacant weight,
The moorland stretches desolate,
And like a wound the sunset bleeds
Across a weary waste of weeds.

A tarn is fed by sluggish rills,
Branching like veins across the hills,
And darkened by a wind that flings
The passing shadow of his wings.

Save where one torture-twisted tree
Shrieks out in silent agony,
Oppressive with its vacant weight,
The moorland stretches desolate.

A grey hawk at a dizzy height
Thrills with its sharp suspended flight,
And like a soft, insidious kiss
The snakes within the heather hiss.

To where as in a monstrous birth
The red moon struggles from the earth,
Oppressive with its vacant weight,
The moorland stretches desolate.

Daisies

The stars are everywhere tonight,
Above, beneath me and around;
They fill the sky with powdery light
And glimmer from the night-strewn ground;
For where the folded daisies are
In every one I see a star.

And so I know that when I pass
Where no sun's shadow counts the hours
And where the sky was there is grass
And where the stars were there are flowers,
Through the long night in which I lie
Stars will be shining in my sky.

The Dead Sparrow

Today I saw a bird
    Lie upturned on the ground;
It seemed as though I found a word
    That had no sound.

Quickly once that sparrow
    Flew rising through the air;
But quicker flew the flying arrow
    That laid it there.

O strange to see it now
    Lying with sidelong head;
Stranger to think it does not know
    Where it lies dead.

That sparrow asks no man
    To dig for it a grave;
Gentle is death, I thought, that can
    Both slay and save.

142

Epitaph
M.F.H.

A flower herself to flowers she went,
Sharer of Beauty's banishment;
She left us winter, but to her
It was the springtime of the year.

The Cobweb

Where idle cobwebs mist the furze
And shake with the least wind that stirs
Their outspread pattern on twig-fork,
Belying the keen spider's work,
Against one trembling web has blown
And struck a starry thistle-down.

Hid in the shadow of a leaf
I see that spider nurse his grief,
A close-hunched ball; content enough
I spring the crafty cobwebs of
My labour and my idleness
To catch a star by its silken tress.

In the New Forest

With branch on sighing branch reclined
    And wild rose beckoning wild rose,
I lose my way, only to find
    That no-one here his way can lose.

Wicken Fen

Nothing is here but sedge-cut skies,
Azure of darting dragon-flies
And horse-flies settling on my flesh
Soft as the touch of spider's mesh.

A plunging pike rocks with a wave
The white-spoked nenuphars that pave
With smooth round leaves the loose-mired lode
That through the fen drives its straight road.

And as the wind blows back the stream
Shaking the buckthorns from their dream,
Time flows back here at Wicken Fen
To swine-steads and blue-woaded men,

Small shaggy men that plunge again
Through sedge and the black rotting rain;
And I too shudder as I feel
The whole earth shake under my heel.

The Flint-Breaker

After the rain was gone
The wind among the trees rained on;
I listening to that scattered tread
Heard what the old flint-breaker said
(Two years or three before):
'Some flints have water at the core.'

Did I walk that sea-bank
Where flints with fluid mouths once drank
The drop they hold apart
In rusty hollow of their heart,
And lingers too in me
One drop of that old Nummulitic Sea?

In Wingfield Manor

As clocklike in the crypt
The water from the stone boughs dripped
And I stood thinking how,
Though it was summer now,
This still was winter rain
Taking so long to drain
That splashed on the earth floor,
Time in a moment slipped
Backward through half a year or more.

Drosera Anglica

Through bogs as black as iodine
    I hunted that fly-catching flower,
Hateful to some, being in fine
    Too like themselves – a carnivore.

Suilven

Throw, Suilven, your dark shadow,
And never let a day go down
Without that monstrous mountain thrown;
For, waking in a darker meadow,
Still your inveterate lover,
I may shake off earth's cover
And flying in ghostly escapade
Mingle your shadow with my colder shade.

Pevensey

With waves that up the shingle shoot
In haste to lick my foot
How false and fawning is the sea,
Like him who crouches on bent knee,
Waiting till bass or ling too late
Discovers the sly bait.

Now as I walk away
Across the flats of Pevensey Bay,
My footsteps on the desert beach
Keeping up a stony speech,
I fear the sea, leaving the shore,
Follows my heel to dog me to my door.

Four Prose Poems

In St Paul's Cathedral

Walking along the choir aisle, I came face to face with the Dean. His eyes were closed, but I thought he gave me a quick glance. He was garbed as on the day he had his picture drawn, his naked body in a shroud with only the face exposed. The picture was intended to be copied in a monument, and the figure I saw is thought to be the monument, which had escaped the Great Fire; but something told me I was seeing the Dean himself, petrified, not for looking back like Lot's wife, but for looking forward, playing the part of a corpse. The figure showed stains of fire, but they were the stains, not of the Great Fire, but of a greater, Purgatory. So now John Donne was in Heaven. 'There we shall all be children of one Quire, and never grow lazie'; in Heaven he was not a Dean, but a well-behaved choir-boy. As a young man he had seen an angel in the sign of the Mermaid Tavern, now he beheld real angels. Did he delight them with his wit? Did he repeat his pun about angels, heavenly beings and gold coins, warning them that some angels could be put on the fire and melted down? Did they call him Jack? Meanwhile his body, which had become its own monument, was still in the cathedral, in the choir aisle, never to return to his great-grand-mother, Dust. His desire had been to die in the pulpit; he had done better, become himself a sermon. How foolishly was a famous Shakespeare passage emended to, 'sermons in books, stones in the running brooks'. 'Sermons in stones' is correct; here was the proof, the most eloquent sermon ever preached in St Paul's.

The Hesperides

Poets have made Hebrides a magic word; sailing for the Outer Isles you hope to light on the Hesperides. The Barra Islands look strange, but they are hills half-sunk in the sea. And once gigantic waves heaving against the six-hundred-foot cliff of Barra Head left small fish on its summit; there are no such storms in the Isles of the Blest. South Uist is mainly rocks, bogs and lochans. The lochans are lively in the wind, tossing white water-lilies and mute swans, but the island has a half-created look, land and water not fully separated and vegetation scarcely begun. Benbecula, its low flat neighbour, appears to be rising from the sea; and it is subject to mirages, a beach tilted like a cliff and off-shore an islet hanging in the air; it is a small piece of creation still unstable. North Uist is even nearer chaos; it has a road, and there are peat-tracks, but you would need wings to explore the watery wilderness. Harris and Lewis are not islands, unless they are Siamese twins. Mountains and long sea-lochs give Harris a grandeur unsuited to human beings, at least more suited to red deer and seals, while in Lewis the Callernish Stones, that in their lonely setting make Stonehenge seem suburban, have a heathenish look; neither could be an Isle of the Blest.

But you need not lose hope of the Hesperides, least of all in North Uist with its Machair Leathann. A machair is merely flat land and a sandy shore, but the one is so verdant and the other so snowy, that spring and winter rub shoulders. The sea only shows itself when it breaks into white ripples; on the beach you step into invisible pools. But some evenings the sea becomes jovial, opal near the shore, turquoise farther out, and where it meets the sky, mocking it with cobalt blue. But that adds nothing to the machair; it takes from it, spoiling the appearance of something fresh from creation, simple and very beautiful. A machair by itself would be a Hesperis.

Near Fowey

From the hills behind Fowey you view a singular sight, mountains of the moon. Cone-shaped and silver, they are entrancing, but the streams that flow from them only a baby would admire. White as milk, they show what the lunar mountains are, the waste-heaps of Cornwall's china clay. Tristan's monument, a longstone standing at a cross-roads, is as tell-tale as the milky streams.

How potent was the love philtre Tristan and Iseult drank; even Hodain, Tristan's hound, became more attached to his master by licking the cup. The jealous Mark thought it less punishment to banish his nephew than to put him to death, but Tristan died a thousand deaths each day. Perhaps Iseult was the truer lover; when he sent her Petitgru, the fairy dog with the golden bell whose tinkling eased the heart of all grief, she flung the bell into the sea. But both died of love; when Iseult, who had the greatest skill in medicine of her time, was summoned to heal Tristan's wounds, 'Tristan died of waiting, Iseult because she came too late'.

But the Tristan monument is tell-tale. Mark was not king of the two countries, Cornwall and England; he was a Celtic chieftain. He did not live at Tintagel in a castle chequered azure and cinnabar, the work of giants; he lived in an earthen camp with a long wooden building, Castle Dor. On the monument, which came from Castle Dor, he is not Tristan's uncle; he is his father! Perhaps the famous romance rose out of nothing more than the sad sound of the name, Tristan. But it would be none the worse for being moonshine like the lunar mountains, waste-heaps of exciting beauty.

Cold Cotswolds

Crocuses in gardens were awake, stretching themselves and yawning; if daffodils are the spring's trumpets, as poets tell us, every garden has its brass band; the flowers even trespassed on public roads. But it was still winter on the wolds; the long lines of beeches were shamelessly naked, shivering in a wind you could see; even violets shivered in their purple hoods. There were no primroses, for those sweet Infantas of the year keep off the cold wolds. I felt coldly towards them myself. But I warmed myself with old memories, of chambered barrows, from the Whispering Knights, a denuded skeleton, to Hetty Pegler's Tump, so far from a skeleton that Hetty looks plump, even pregnant. And with memories of buildings in the Tudor tradition, from manor-houses with an ambiguity as to what they are, domestic or ecclesiastical, to small houses that have a dignity that makes you feel inferior to their owners; the Royal Family could live in Chipping Campden's alms-houses.

But the cold Cotswolds added a new memory. Driving over the Edge in twilight, I saw what was apocalyptic. Dark cloud shadowed the sky and the Severn Valley lay in deep shade, but between cloud and shadow burned a sunset, a long sea of fire. There, if anywhere, were 'the flaming ramparts of the world'. Or was I seeing farther, not a sunset, but a sunrise on another world? No, it was too lurid; it was a reflection from some infernal region. And I was hastening down to it, leaving not only the Cotswolds, but the earth itself. Drawing closer to my companion, the sharer of old memories, I said silently,

> You have so much forgiven,
> Forgive me this or that, or Hell or Heaven.